Post Traumatic Stress Disorder and Dramatherapy

Treatment and Risk Reduction

Linda Winn

Jessica Kingsley Publishers
London and Bristol, Pennsylvania

First published in the United Kingdom in 1994 by
Jessica Kingsley Publishers Ltd
116 Pentonville Road, London N1 9JB, England
and
1900 Frost Road, Suite 101
Bristol, PA 19007, U S A

Copyright © 1994 Linda Winn

Library of Congress Cataloging in Publication Data
Winn, Linda (Linda Caroline). 1957-
Post-traumatic stress disorder and dramatherapy: treatment and
risk-reduction/Linda Winn
p. cm
Includes bibliographical references and index.
ISBN 1-85302-183-0 (pbk.)
1. Post-traumatic stress disorder – Treatment. 2. Psychodrama
3. Post-traumatic stress disorder – Prevention. I. Title.
RC552.P67W56 1994
616.85'21–dc20

British Library Cataloguing in Publication Data
Winn, Linda
Post Traumatic Stress Disorder
and Dramatherapy: Treatment and
Risk Reduction
I. Title
616.8913

ISBN 1-85302-183-0

Printed and Bound in Great Britain by
Biddles Ltd., Guildford and King's Lynn

or before

Post Traumatic Stress Disorder and Dramatherapy

Treatment and Risk Reduction

of related interest

Storymaking in Education and Therapy
Alida Gersie and Nancy King
ISBN 1 85302 519 4 hb
ISBN 1 85302 520 8 pb

Storymaking in Bereavement
Dragons Fight in the Meadow
Alida Gersie
ISBN 1 85302 065 6 hb
ISBN 1 85302 176 8 pb

Art Therapy and Dramatherapy
Masks of the Soul
Sue Jennings and Åse Minde
ISBN 1 85302 027 3

Focus on Psychodrama
The Therapeutic Aspects of Psychodrama
Peter Felix Kellermann
Foreword by Jonathon D Moreno
ISBN 1 85302 127 X

Contents

To my children,
Andrew and Rosie

Acknowledgements

I would like to thank all those who have given encouragement and support to me, both in my work and in the writing of this book: without their help it would not have been possible. I wish to pay tribute to those whose journeys I have been honoured to share in and whose lives have touched mine: although more often than not we then go on our separate ways, I take with me some lasting essence of the experience.

The staff at the Unit at the Royal Naval Hospital (Haslar), in particular Morgan O'Connell, Una and Bob together with the PTSD Course members who taught me so much and also reminded me of the importance of laughter in life – thanks for helping me to feel at home in a strange land.

Jessica Kingsley and Helen Skelton for their advice and work in guiding me through to publication. Alida Gersie for finding the time to write the Foreword and for her original encouragement to submit the work that I have been doing in order that it be shared with a wider audience.

Finally I would like to thank and express my appreciation to those authors and publishers who have given permission for me to quote from their work – they are listed in detail in the references. I need to give special mention to William Horwood (*Duncton Found*) and Russell Hoban (*The Dancing Tigers*) who have allowed their storytelling to be used in this context and for the stories themselves which continue to inspire and strengthen me.

The identifying features of all therapeutic material have been changed to preserve anonymity.

Foreword

When William James first spoke of 'thorns of the spirit', he referred to those reminiscences of shock which are half forgotten, yet linger.[1] The shock of horrific experiences and their subsequent trauma reaction need acknowledgement, for once denied they trigger further difficulties and may later be reconstituted under the diagnostic label of anxiety neurosis, a morbid nervous condition, or, more recently, Post Traumatic Stress Disorder (PTSD). These are the embodied thorns of the spirit.[2]

Severe trauma alters our experience of reality, suddenly and against our will. We saw what we were not ready to see, heard what we were unable to hear, and smelled what we are unable to describe. Words were not big enough to convey what it was like to live through these circumstances. Yet our wellbeing depends on our capacity to express the feelings which accompany the traumatic experience, such as anxiety, hyper vigilance, depression and temporary paranoid ideation. None of these reactions to trauma constitutes pathology *per se*. Our sobs, screams, moans are ordinary reactions to unexpected, severe pain.

The good thing is that not all traumas develop into PTSD. Often friends, colleagues and relatives are able to hear the story of what happened to someone in their midst.[3] They listen again and again. Such people are able to tolerate the upsurge of their own painful memories, can contain their outrage and fear, and offer the suffering person the necessary support during those roller-coaster weeks or months that follow profound traumatization. Unintimidated by the emotional turmoil that accompanies every recovery, they gradually

1   James, W., (1898) in *Psychology Review I*, p.199.
2   Everstine, D.S., Everstine, L., (1993) *People in Crisis: Strategic Therapeutic Interventions*. New York: Brunner/Mazel.
3   Kleinman, A. (1988) *The Illness Narratives: Suffering, Healing and the Human Condition*. New York: Basic Books.

help the trauma-victim to rebuild some kind of faith in life and nourish a renewed capacity for self-soothing and self-care which were lost when trouble hit.

However, not everyone is this lucky. Trauma also comes to those people whose intimate life is not in great shakes, whose employment situation is not supportive, and whose friends cannot bear to hear the details of what happened. In addition, many people who work in the police force, in medicine, social or rescue services or for railway companies have built into their daily work shocking encounters with pain, mutilation and assault. Their stories too need voicing, although the support necessary to enable this in a professional context is all too frequently unavailable.

It is self evident that following trauma a person's entry into recovery will take time and that there are various stages to this process. The first priority in any acute stage of trauma will be to stabilize the situation and de-pathologize the responses, to foster mastery and reduce the felt sense of profound isolation.[4] Somehow a degree of connection with an average kind of reality needs to be restored, which later needs to incorporate full awareness of the horrors that happened.[5]

In this process of recovery pharmacotherapy sometimes plays a useful role. The power of modern pharmaceuticals cannot be denied and yet, their virtues need to be extremely carefully considered in the context of the risks of long-term dependency in which the acute traumatic crisis is never transcended, but merely translated into a prolonged period of maintenance treatment. In addition, it must not be forgotten that the medical impairment of traumatized people may contra-indicate chemical treatment. Therefore, where possible, effective nonchemical therapeutic procedures which aid recovery from emotional distress, must be the preferred treatment strategy, pro-

---

4   Coyne, J.C. and Segal, L. (1982) A Brief Strategic Interactional
      Approach to Psychotherapy. In Anchin, J.C. and Kiesler, D.J. (eds)
      Handbook of Interpersonal Psychotherapy. Pergamon, p.248–261.
5   Makari, G., and Shapiro, T. (1993) On psychological listening:
      language and unconscious communication, *Journal of the American
      Psychoanalytic Association*. Vol 41 No 4, 991–1020.

vided they offer a very genuine option to alleviate pain and to support healing.[6]

Mental health workers such as nurse-therapists, social workers, psychologists, probation officers and occupational therapists, already use a wide range of methods and exercises to reduce the impact of anxiety and other emotional difficulties, such as relaxation methods, guided imagery activities, eye-movement desensitization and reprocessing procedures, meditation, breathing techniques, massage and physical exercises, distractors in the form of drawing or games, explorations of life-philosophy, dramatizations, recreational activities, and the building of an intimate relationship with pets. The effectiveness of such individual techniques has been well documented and researched.[7]

Although not strong on pets and dolphins, it might, at first glance, seem that the techniques repertoire most commonly used in the creative arts therapies (music therapy, art therapy, dance movement therapy, dramatherapy and poetry therapy) incorporates several of the above, as indeed it does.[8]

The vital difference, however, is that the creative arts therapist, and therefore the dramatherapist's practice, is guided by the aim to help a person to (re-) gain use of specific artistic processes for the purpose of healing, and by the training and know-how to achieve this. Susan Langer wrote that the function of art is to acquaint the beholder with something he had not known before.[9] In arts therapy practice, inner experience which has been partly forgotten, yet which is felt as insurmountable suffering, is made expressible and perceptible through the purposeful use of specific art forms such as dramatization and storytelling. The client is helped to become both creator and beholder of his or her life that was, in this specific form, not known before. Therefore the art of dramatherapy involves the struc-

6   Rosenthal, T.L (1993) To soothe the savage breast, *Behaviour Research and Therapy*, Vol 31, No 5, 439–462.
7   Kanfer, F.H. and Goldstein, A.P. (eds) (1991) *Helping People Change. 4th edition.* Pergamon.
8   Aldridge, D., Brandt, G. and Wohler, D. (1990) Toward a common language in the arts therapies, *The Arts in Psychotherapy*, Vol 17, 189–195.
9   Langer, S. (1953) *Feeling and Form: A Theory of Art.* London: Routledge and Kegan Paul.

turing of the dramatic experience in such a way that it embodies both an expression of the current situation and the means to transcend it. Through the conscious and informed use of this dual process of healing (cathartic and transformative) the explicit or disguised thorns of the spirit may be healed. Research by Cattanach, Jennings, Johnson, Lahad and Landy supports the contention that it is not only useful to have access to such a place where the truth of one's experience can be dramatically expressed and responded to honestly, it may be vital.

When we are traumatized our background world, our world of reference 'before it happened', as one of my clients once said, with its pre-existing sets of properties, must change in order to accommodate and to incorporate the now lived reality of traumatic occurances. The creation of imagined subworlds, in which the therapist and client join in flexible interplay between the roles of performer and witness, helps the clients to explore imaginatively those beliefs, hopes, fears, commands and wishes which were fundamentally challenged due to the experience of profound trauma.[10]

In dramatherapy the structure of the experience of trauma and trauma-reaction is given form, and thereby separated, emphasized, sung about in intensity and reintegrated. When all the world seems lost and changed, and the inevitable has become utterly hopeless, we need such hypothetical dramatic worlds. Not just a world of everlasting sorrow and misery, nor the everlasting world of 'all will be well', but one where we explore our anger, grief and tenderness in due course in our own time in unusual ways, so that spontaneity and discovery once more come within benign reach.

The weakness of any method which is circumscribed by a set of techniques is that it might appear to offer a limited number of standard formats, combined with the feeding of a diet of relentless optimism.[11] The creative arts therapies in general, and dramatherapy in particular, with their emphasis on creative productivity, do indeed play a significant role in the fostering of hope. Above all,

---

10   Eco, U. (1978) Possible worlds and text pragmatics: un drama bien parisien, *Versus*, 5–72.
        Elam, K. (1991) *The Semiotics of Theatre and Drama*. London: Routledge.
11   Efran, J.S. and Schenker, M.D. (1993) A potpourri of solutions, *The Family Therapy Networker*, May/June, 71–74.

however, dramatherapy offers the client an opportunity to redis-cover himself or herself by expressing the lived past, within the containment offered by a structured aesthetic framework, in the presence of a truly listening and informed other person.

Dramatic activities offer such elusive qualities as joy, satisfaction, delighted surprise. We see them when expressed in action. Engage-ment in the very process of constructing a story or drama (rather than having a constructed story *per se*) is predictive of health and recovery of health, partly because we express ourselves linguistically and biologically at the same time. We cannot not do so, even though, when 'our life is warped past cure', we feel that we are in a state of torn-to-pieces-ness. Shakespeare always knew that in this state our words and movements and relationships fall into disarray – a disar-ray that can be addressed through the very means which made it happen: embodied action.

When we express ourselves creatively we bear witness. This is so even when we would like to create a false impression, like we do when putting a brave face on things. When this desire 'to hide and through hiding to unveil' is purposefully worked with in dramatherapy, it arouses a wide range of emotions. Some of these are difficult and painful. In the long run, however, the act of psycho-logically confronting emotionally upsetting events is associated with improved physical and psychological health. As Pennebaker says: 'Shakespeare implicitly knew this. And now, after hundreds of hours of research, we know it as well.'[12]

This book describes some techniques derived from the arts thera-pies, and particularly dramatherapy, that Linda Winn has found useful in treating people who needed care for Post Traumatic Stress Disorder. She offers the 'front line' practitioner, who is willing to be present to the sombre effects of profound trauma, some ways for-ward, and down-to-earth counsel. It is a book that stays close to the daily reality of life in our hospitals, clinics and social services centres. At times the author speaks a language of tough care as well as substantial tenderness. Through straightforward description of her

---

12   Pennebaker, J.W. (1993) Putting stress into words: health, linguistics and therapeutic implications, *Behaviour Research and Therapy*, Vol 31, No 6, 539–548.

own practice she encourages other mental health practitioners to bear emotional and imaginative witness, thereby to help people to work through their terrible experiences.

Trauma involves very real damage, an encounter with suffering that cannot be undone. Then one has, as Victor Frankl writes, a chance to activate life's highest value, to fulfil the deepest meaning, the meaning of suffering.[13] By writing onto paper, or forming as sound or dramatic action our possible answers to life's urgent questions, we travel beyond the stuckness of profound distress, slowly moving towards a renewed consent, which embraces the challenge to our humanity which was encountered in the trauma-experience.

It is a difficult and gradual journey, but a possible one, and that is a great deal more than most people believe after experiencing trauma.

Alida Gersie
Palo Alto
March 1994

---

13   Frankl, V. (1963) *Man's Search for Meaning.* New York: Washington Square Press.

CHAPTER 1

What is Post Traumatic Stress Disorder?

It was a black, a bitter and a brutal time, and I suppose that this huge chronicle of injustice, ugliness and suffering, gained an added darkness.

Thomas Wolfe
The Autobiography of an American Novelist

Post Traumatic Stress Disorder has been given the following diagnostic criteria in the American Psychiatric Association's *Diagnostic Statistical Manual of Mental Disorders* (1987):

1. The experience of an abnormal stressor.
2. The re-experiencing of the event (flashbacks).
3. Avoidance behaviour. (The sufferer seeks to avoid situations which may trigger memories of the event.)
4. Increased arousal to stimuli (e.g. certain smell, sounds, sights associated with the incident may provoke a physical reaction such as nausea, panic etc.).
5. A duration of more than one month.

In cases of PTSD the following are in evidence:

1. A recognised stressor. (An incident to which the current difficulty is directly attributable.)
2. A re-experiencing of the event.
3. A numbing of responsiveness (this can be very distressing, for example, recalling a motor accident but only seeing empty vehicles with no helpers or others involved).

In addition, at least two of the following symptoms were not present before the traumatising event:

1. Hyper-alertness.
2. Sleep disturbance.
3. Survivor or performance guilt ('I should have done that differently').
4. Memory or concentration problems.
5. Avoidance behaviour.
6. Intensification: a widening of tension and anxiety to other areas.

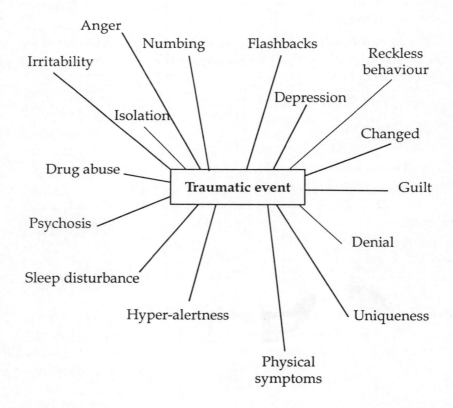

Figure 1.1: Physical Symptoms of Post-Traumatic Stress Disorder

What is special about Post-Traumatic Stress?

It is not uncommon for Post Traumatic Stress to be confused with other forms of stress, and cases have been known in which professionals have attempted to treat a sufferer of PTSD in the same way as they might approach a generalised stress condition. If practitioners are searching for a familiar model to help them identify similarities in clients reactions, it may be helpful to consider a model of stages of grief in loss and bereavement (see also Further Reading):

Stage 1: Shock, denial

Stage 2: The acknowledgement (not necessarily acceptance) of the loss

Stage 3: Depression

Stage 4: Acceptance, healing

It is common for people to move from one of these stages to another, in no fixed order, throughout their grieving process.

Whilst there are some common symptoms between PTSD and other forms of stress, such as physiological arousal (see Chapter 5) and problems with memory and concentration, the major difference is that in PTSD the sufferer has experienced an incident which is outside the normal life pattern. In the initial stages following this event there is a normal reaction to the abnormal experience – PTSD develops at a later stage, usually after approximately one month.

A person who is under stress as a result of work or lifestyle can be encouraged to modify their behaviour and activities. Taking a break or a holiday might also be of benefit in such cases. However, it is most unlikely that any of this would be of much worth to somebody who is psychologically traumatised and haunted by what has happened to them!

PTSD is about loss at a severe and serious level and can be the result of both very public and very private events. It is not necessarily connected with death or injury, or any external form of deprivation, but it can involve the loss of self-worth, self-respect, meaning to life, and faith. This loss requires expression or acknowledgement in order that the person may be able to move on with their journey through life.

After a major disaster

PTSD may often be found in victims of a major disaster, such as war, terrorist attacks, fires, major accidents, floods, and so on, and it may be intensified by the focus of media attention and public information. Such events are peculiar in a number of ways that may make the reactions of those who experience them very different from any other kind of grief reaction. These peculiarities are:

1. The event is publicly scrutinised and analysed. Scapegoats and heroes are created and anniversaries are commemorated, placing much – and often long-term – pressure on those involved.

2. It is a 'mass' event. The dead are mixed up with the living, it is overwhelming – outside the range of normal experience. As Accident and Emergency Departments go on red alert, triage is carried out in order to deal as fast as possible with the severely injured, which, by its selection process of numbering, adds to the de-humanising experience.

3. Helpers are unprepared.

4. Strong countertransference may take place between workers and those affected, leading to workers becoming traumatised.

After a more 'private' incident

There are, in addition, many people who experience PTSD after a more private event. Just a few such examples are people who have been mugged or raped, sexually assaulted in other ways, burgled, held hostage, involved in a car accident, or witnessed a murder or suicide. In such cases, there is unlikely to be as much media attention as in the aftermath of major disasters – although it may make headlines briefly – and anniversaries of the event will be quickly forgotten by most members of the public. As a result, the sufferer may feel more isolated and under increased pressure to 'get back to normal'.

It is unlikely that psychological debriefing will be offered at the time. Some General Practitioners do recognise that there is a possibility of Post Traumatic Stress and arrange assessment or further treatment; however, many people report asking their doctor for help and being told that things would improve in a few weeks and to go away and try to forget about it. People may only be referred after they have expressed fears that they are 'losing their minds' – it can come as a great relief to them to hear that they are actually experiencing a normal reaction to what has happened.

In such cases, there may also be additional complications such as pending legal cases: the individual may be a defendant awaiting compensation or may be being prosecuted for some suspected negligence. The arrival of solicitors' letters, often several years after the event, can be particularly distressing and re-open old wounds. In Britain it appears to take, in many cases, around five years for any resolution to come about through the Courts, and those involved are less likely to have support through this than those involved in a mass incident where self-help and support groups are often set up. Relatives of those affected are also isolated, as they are usually unable to compare notes with other families trying to make sense of their loved one's behaviour.

Who is at risk from Post Traumatic Stress?

There has yet to be much research done into predisposing personality traits or other factors that may increase the risk of suffering from PTSD. It may be helpful to think about groups that should be considered following any traumatic incident, for example:

- the victims and their 'significant others'
- witnesses
- those who 'should have been there'
- front-line staff, such as Rescue Services and Accident and Emergency personnel
- the hidden affected, such as switchboard operators, cleaners, porters, volunteer helpers and journalists.

This list is not exhaustive, but illustrates the far reaching 'ripple' effect that an abnormal event can cause.

In her book *When Disaster Strikes* (1986), Raphael differentiates between man-made and natural disaster, suggesting that recovery from natural disaster is faster. However, there are many variables to be considered, such as the fact that in many natural disasters there are few survivors and entire communities may have been wiped out. She presents the following findings:

Morbidity levels

20–70%	of victims experience psychological symptoms in the first week after the traumatising event. There is a significant drop after ten weeks.
30–40%	experience psychological symptoms in the first year.
30–70%	continue to experience disturbance during the second year, particularly if the incident was man-made and there was a high rate of shock (for example, from unexpectedness)
20%	are thought still to be affected in the second year if the disturbance was caused by natural disaster.

In practice, I have found that those who have strong, supportive family or social networks seem less likely to develop PTSD and, if they do, seek help at an earlier stage of the illness, often having been persuaded to do so by significant others. This is in the process of being researched, however, and no conclusions can yet be made.

It is not unusual for someone who has been dealing with trauma for much of their working life (such as ambulance staff) suddenly to have a profound reaction to a single incident or a run of traumatic incidents. It is almost as if they become 'super saturated' to the point where they have to say 'no more' – if not verbally then by actions such as avoidance and withdrawal both in their work and social lives. There is often a reluctance to admit to any difficulties, perhaps even more so when there are career implications. It is to be hoped that, as more people are made aware of both the possibility of PTSD and the fact that the risks can be reduced, employers will take pro-active steps to ensure that support networks, separate from the management structure, are readily available. Many of the people I have worked with who have been diagnosed as suffering from PTSD are conscientious, highly trained and caring individuals who, given the right help, could exercise their choice to return to the work-force, thereby preventing a valuable resource being lost.

The National Union of Public Employees submission to the Hillsborough Inquiry (1991) highlighted the stress that staff undergo when tragedies such as Hillsborough are added to the pressure of their routine work. Facing the horrific problems of these situations has an adverse affect on even the most experienced and hardened staff. The report showed that stress was evident after the event was over, when staff had time to reflect on the situation and NUPE recommended that the government, after consultation with the trade unions and employers, set up a body to provide immediate professional help upon which employers could call to provide counselling facilities for staff. An ACAS (1989) report into the London Ambulance Service concluded that 'routine emergency calls, but particularly more critical ones such as the death of a child or difficult extractions from a Road Traffic Accident had cumulative strain consequences for crews'.

There now seems to be a general recognition in all areas, including employers and managers, trade unions and occupational health workers, of factors which may contribute to PTSD and even the possible cessation of employment for skilled staff; however, there is still a reluctance on the part of many employers to implement risk-reduction methods or make early help easily available.

People referred for assessment will not necessarily present the same symptoms. For example, in an attempt to regain control of their lives and to avoid distressing thoughts, they may develop one of a variety of maladaptive coping responses, such as violent behaviour, alcoholism, lawbreaking, putting their own or others' lives at risk (fast driving or playing 'chicken'), the development of an eating disorder (which provides something they feel they can control), or a psychosis.

Whatever form of therapy one is going to offer, it is important that a careful history of the client is taken. It is not unusual to find that someone who has reacted badly to a traumatic event is also re-experiencing a previous trauma that has remained repressed for many years. For example, a woman was admitted to hospital for psychiatric treatment following a mugging in which she was robbed of her purse. She left the hospital and was found by railway police sitting on a platform and attempting to mutilate her genitalia. In the lengthy treatment and support that followed it emerged that she had been raped by a 'friend' of the family when she was nine years old, had told no-one about it for fear of her life and had attempted to rectify what had happened to her by obsessional behaviour – she had become extremely neat and had developed various rituals in order to 'protect' herself. Her belief was that by doing all this, all would be well in her life. Until the mugging at the age of twenty, her experience had reinforced this belief: she was academically successful, had a boyfriend whom she loved and found sexually pleasing and she was popular in her social setting. Suddenly, however, the mugging left her value system shattered and her rituals of no use. It is common in such cases for crisis to occur as a strong reaction to an old wound which has been left untreated, and is deteriorating and chronic.

In treating this woman it was important to proceed slowly, in order to prevent her trying once more to submerge herself in denial and avoidance (with the resulting emergence of psychotic behaviour) and to give her support as she worked through this stage of her journey and to enable her to move on. It required a team approach and shared aims from the people involved in her care. It is important for the primary or key worker/therapist working with someone suffering from PTSD to ensure that the other staff involved are aware of how they are working and the treatment plan agreed between the worker and the client. The team, as bystanders able to offer helpful observations and comments, can then be supportive of both parties.

Conclusion

This chapter has given a brief insight into what PTSD is and who may be affected by it. The key points to remember are:

- PTSD is defined as 'the development of certain characteristic symptoms following a psychologically distressing event which is outside the range of normal human experience' (APA 1987).

- PTSD can arise following a major disaster where many people have been affected, or after a more personal, intimate event that leaves an individual or a small group of people traumatised.

- A poor support network, a lack of anyone to provide information or aid understanding of what is occurring and a failure of previously learnt coping mechanisms may also contribute to the occurrence of PTSD.

- People who have not been psychologically debriefed following a traumatic incident are more likely to go on to develop PTSD or seek help because they do not understand what is happening to them and fear they may be losing their mind.

It is essential for the dramatherapist to be aware of these factors before proceeding with the treatment outlined in this book – it is only then that the therapist is in a position to provide education and information on this subject to the client. This is a big step in reducing their fears and anxieties about what they are experiencing.

If the trauma is recent, the therapy may be complete once debriefing has taken place. However, this book will take you through the process of using dramatherapy both in debriefing and in treatment strategies. It is hoped that the non-dramatherapist may also find a useful framework within which to work.

Further reading

Burgess, A.W. and Baldwin, A.B. (1981) *Crisis Intervention Theory and Practice*. New Jersey: Prentice-Hall International Inc.

Horowitz, M.J., Wilner, N., Kaltreider, N. and Alvarez, W. (1980) 'Signs and Symptoms of Post Traumatic Stress Disorder'. *Archives of General Psychiatry, 37 (1)*, 85–93.

Kübler-Ross, E. (1969) *On Death and Dying*. New York: MacMillan.

Leick, N. and Davidsen-Nielsen, M. (1991) *Healing Pain: Attachment, Loss and Grief Therapy*. London: Routledge.

NIMH Diagnostic Interviews Schedule-Version 111. Public Health Service, publication ADM -T-42–3 (5–8–81). Rockville, MD: NIMH.

CHAPTER 2

Normalisation

When autumn passes then must winter numb,
And winter may not pass a weary while,
But when it passes spring shall flower again:
And in that spring who weepeth now shall smile.

Christina Rossetti

It is thought that an important factor in preventing breakdown after a traumatic event is 'normalisation'. It has become practice to provide those involved in incidents such as the King's Cross fire with cards containing information on what feelings and symptoms it is *normal* to experience following such an event (see Figure 1.1, p.2). In addition a helpline is usually provided for those seeking further reassurance. Staff who have worked on such helplines can confirm that that callers often ask such questions as 'I'm having bad dreams still, is that normal?', and when reassured that it is, are satisfied and ring off.

Figure 2.1 shows information given to some people returning from the Gulf War. In preparation for this, and now in some areas as part of basic training, people were taught about Battle Stress and the normal reactions that can be expected as a response to trauma. There is an on-going debate as to whether alerting people to various symptoms is beneficial: one argument is that mentioning symptoms may unnecessarily alarm people and subsequently cause them to develop those that have been described. However, I believe that information should be made available to people: if professionals keep such information to themselves it can put them in an unfairly powerful position (Guggenbuhl 1971).

It is important that the information provided is accurate. In recent years many people have probably learnt about PTSD through media

Whilst in the Gulf you are likely to have been involved in a particular incident, or series of incidents, which have been outside the range of usual human experience. People often experience one or more problems in settling down to daily life in the first few weeks following such incidents. During this time, it is normal to dream about the incident, to feel suddenly that it is happening again whilst awake, to try to avoid reminders of the incident, and to react strongly (by sweating or feeling sick for example) when reminded of the incident. It is also normal to lose interest in present and future events and in other people, even loved ones, to have difficulty in sleeping and concentration, to overreact to everyday difficulties and to feel generally irritable, 'wound up' and 'jumpy'.

You might experience some of these or other problems during the first few weeks. Although the experience will be far from pleasant, try not to worry, as the problems are likely to become fewer as days go by and you will gradually readjust to life around you. However, we are providing you with a helpline card should you wish to talk to someone.

Helpline

If you require advice or assistance following your recent experiences in the Gulf, please contact the number given below. Either a member of the Department will take your call or you can leave a message on the answering machine and we will return your call as soon as possible.

Figure 2.1: Text from a leaflet given to those returning from the Gulf War

reports, some of which have been educational and valuable while others have been hyped and alarmist. Many of the people I have worked with have expressed regret, and sometimes anger, that they were not informed at an early stage that the emotions they were experiencing were normal. Ninety per cent expressed a fear that they were going mad, and in many cases this fear had caused them to isolate themselves and internalise thoughts and fears. If the method of more education to stress the normality of reactions continues, research may show a decrease in the number of those who go on to develop PTSD, although it is not possible to predict whether outcomes will be different.

This kind of information should also be extended to relatives and key workers in the community, whether they are statutory or voluntary. They will often be the people closest to those affected and in the best position to offer support. If they are aware of which symptoms are normal, then they will be less likely to react with alarm. There is a danger that professionals, in their wish to help, will wrest responsibility and independence from a community following an incident, rather than making use of resources already there. As professional support does eventually stop, leaving both individuals and communities to their own devices, it is preferable that they have been allowed to discover the strengths and gifts that they have, in order to help themselves to cope. Individuals who do develop PTSD in the future will need skilled specific help.

The following account of the way in which someone who had been involved in a traumatic event moved on from his experience is useful when considering the concept of normalisation. It is worth mentioning the writer's comment that perhaps his contribution to this book would be his final 'laying of the ghosts'.

> That year, Boxing Day had been on the Thursday and with three busy racing days at the end of the Christmas week, we had kept the money in the office safe.

> I was managing one of the larger betting shops of a medium size group in the outer London area. Although most of our regular business came from the small factories and workshops on the industrial estate where the shop was situated, we were close to a very heavily populated sprawl of flats and terraced houses.

> It had been a successful (for the bookmaker) holiday period, and by close of business on Saturday I had locked over £2000 in our new multi-combination 1.5-ton safe. The cashiers had

gone home, and Bert and I were having a final tidy-up before getting back to our respective family festivities.

Bert was my assistant manager and board-man (long before the days of television screens in the shops, these were the people who marked up the prices and results on the 'board' as they were broadcast over the Extel system). A pleasant, friendly, man in his late forties, about 15 years older than me, Bert was waiting for his wife to collect him in the family car, just as she did most days after work.

There was a knock on the outside door and, seeing her face pressed up against the reinforced frosted glass panel, I unlocked the door.

Pam was thrust headlong into the shop. She had been grabbed by two men when she got out of her car. One of them had forced her to the door and, as I opened it, they threw her forwards and rushed in behind her. Both were brandishing handguns – one held what looked like a small automatic pistol and the other had a Luger.

With a very fast reaction, Bert dived behind the counter and grabbed the pickaxe handle which was there for 'emergencies'. None of the shops had ever needed to use this blunt instrument and I couldn't see it being too appropriate in the present circumstances.

'Put it down Bert – they've got guns...' I still remember that phrase, or at least I remember the memory of it after more than twenty years. I also recall how unreal and farcical the whole situation seemed.

The two gunmen were as terrified as the rest of us. They each wore balaclava helmets and had blackened their faces (when they came close their presence was accentuated by an overpowering smell of boot polish). Shaking visibly, one pointed his pistol at my head and ordered me into the back office where the safe stood defiantly visible to the shop. 'Open it,' he growled, 'or you're dead.' In a kneeling position, I began to fumble with the delicate combination lock. It was not a good time to remember something like: 4 left 23–3 right 16–2 left 37

– 1 right 26, especially as we change the combination every few weeks and this had only been done just before the holiday. My hands trembled. I missed the number and had to start again. The other robber became agitated. Still levelling his weapon at Bert and Pam, he switched off the main shop lights. This also turned out the office illumination. I missed the number again. A click at my ear sounded like the safety catch. In true 1940s movie style came the snarl: 'If you're stalling, you're a dead man.'

I had had enough. These characters had a bloody cheek – and they were incompetent. Dangerous too – but even more so because they were a shambles. My outburst was not bravery – not even bravado. It was adrenalin plus exasperation. 'Look, you can have the money. I am not paid to put up with this. But I can't operate the combination with you sticking that in my neck and I can't open the safe in the effin' dark!'

They stood back to let me get on with it, and shovelled the notes and large silver into linen bank bags. One of them produced a ball of parcel twine and ordered us to lie down on the shop floor. Whilst his companion stood pointing both pistols at us, he bound us tightly with the thin, tough, flesh-cutting string. Our knees were bent with our ankles tied behind our wrists before they finally stepped back. 'Sorry about this,' muttered the one who had done the tying, 'but we've had a bad Christmas. Don't try moving for half an hour. We could still be outside waiting for our motor.'

That was probably the worst part of the entire episode for me. Trussed as we were face down, I fully expected a kick in the head to render us unconscious and to make it that much safer for our assailants. But the kick never came. One went into the office and ripped the telephone from the wall. The other put the smaller pistol on the counter and said: 'It's only a toy gun. We'll leave it so the law can see it wasn't real.' They didn't leave the Luger behind.

We lay there for a few minutes after the door had closed. In the shadow of the one security light we verified that we were all physically unharmed. It took Bert about ten minutes to wriggle free. They had made a better job of my bonds, but he cut me loose and while he helped his wife, I put the bolt across the door and went back into the office. It was the shop's intercom which had been torn out. The outside telephone, on a ledge behind the desk, was still working.

I dialled 999 and, once connected to the police, still in keeping with the gangster vernacular, I excitedly advised the listening officer that this was the Western Road betting shop and we had been 'done over'. 'Done over, sir? What exactly do you mean, and could we begin by having your name please...' That was it – back to cold reality. As the centre stage of the 'B' movie set faded with the arrival of uniformed policemen, CID and 'Scene of Crime' officers, and my boss, we became involved in the process of making laborious and tedious statements. I telephoned my wife who was convinced that I had stopped off for another festive drink and was making yet another, albeit unusually inventive, excuse for being late home.

Seasonal cheer was indeed provided by the boss, who produced two bottles of scotch from his car boot which he generously shared out with the investigator of the crime. I have clear recollections of being excluded from the friendly invitations to freely imbibe. Apart from a muttered comment when he first arrived, asking me if this was so I could make a down payment on a cottage in Devon, my employer virtually ignored the three of us, who could so easily have suffered injury or death for the sake of his money.

A reward was offered. The local newspapers livened up their New Year issues, but the robbers were never apprehended. A few weeks later there was a similar raid on a betting shop in Shepherd's Bush. The owner put up a fight. He was shot and killed. As far as I know the murderer was not caught.

I left the area in that new year and moved my family to Cornwall, where we rented a house in a peaceful village, and I went to train on the Home Office Probation and Child Care Officer course. I did not buy a country cottage.

For a while I kept in touch with Bert. He stayed with the firm and seemed to get over the incident fairly quickly, but Pam had a bad time throughout the months which followed. Nightmares, nervousness, episodes of uncontrollable shaking, sickness, loss of appetite. It sounded from Bert's phone calls and letters that the only way this was eventually controlled was by high doses of prescribed tranquillisers.

How did I deal with it? In a way, I suppose I am still dealing with it. More than twenty years ago, and I still talk about it. I have used the experience to illustrate trauma – impact – recoil – adjustment. Depending upon the listener and the circumstances I have made the incident a point of discussion across the spectrum, ranging from light-hearted after dinner chat, highlighting any amusing aspects ('we've had a bad Christmas' – switching off lights while victim tries desperately to unlock combination safe), to criminology seminars linking into murder as the end result of armed robbery.

There was no effort of recall, no struggle to edit this written account. I was easily able to respond to the invitation to record this episode by simply taking pen to paper and allowing memories to flow.

Other examples of violence and threats have crossed my path in the subsequent years. As a mental welfare officer, I faced threats of knives, shotguns (loaded), another Luger (its one bullet fired into the ceiling, but we didn't know at the time there were none to follow!) As a child care officer and social worker, there were various occupational hazards of irate and violent clients, wildly angry parents at times, and the potential suicide who refused to let me leave his caravan, which he had packed with vast quantities of weeping gelignite. Then, only four or five years ago, when I was a prospective Parliamentary candidate, I received a death threat postcard. I hadn't been too worried about that until I saw how seriously the police and Special Branch treated it.

My way of coping with it all has been to talk about it – to write about it in reports, in articles, in letters to the press, to family, to friends, and to colleagues.

No sleepless nights (except the odd one or two immediately after the different experiences), no bad dreams (except the odd one or two), no residual nervous problems (if you don't count digestive and stomach disorders). Just a lot of tolerant and generous friends and acquaintances and long-suffering family, who must be very weary from hearing the same stories so many times over the years.

Storytelling

Storytelling, as documented elsewhere (Gersie 1983 1991, Gersie and King 1990), is very useful during the process of normalisation, as it facilitates the use of an abstract structured approach. The abstract nature of the story allows the reader or listener to maintain a distance while absorbing the metaphors as they apply to their situation. They may identify with a particular character, event or emotion, and it is common for different aspects of the story to resonate at different times. As part of the normalisation process, the sharing of stories with adults or children is another way of saying 'it's okay – you're okay'. Alida Gersie (1991), for example, recounts the story of a coyote and an eagle in the land of the dead, which displays many of the elements present in acute grieving – personal neglect, denial, magical thinking and searching, and the fruitless efforts of helpers to try and make things better.

Another example is the use that survivors of sexual abuse have made of the children's story *The Dancing Tigers* (Hoban 1979). In this story the tigers are resigned to their fate of being hunted and killed because that was the way it had always been. One day the Hunter adds another dimension to the ritual of the hunt, 'light classics'. For the tigers, this is the last straw, and it provokes them to review their situation. The tigers have been pushed to the limit and use resources they already have to retaliate. They no longer see themselves as victims and instead create an alternative future. In abusive relationships, change often only takes place when the victim's tolerance level has been exceded.

According to Nira Kfir (1989, p.20):

If crisis is a disruption of balance, then the function of intervention is to help to restore it by recruiting the victim's own particular coping style... we recognised an additional dimension to crisis. That dimension is to understand it as process. The start of a crisis means disengaging the automatic pilot. Its absence is dreaded and the victim anxious to get back to normal life. However, if we can relate to crisis as being part of the normal process of life, then we, as observers, can see this as a 'time off' period, a possible transition and a potential transformation. We can then step back and allow the process to open up the possibility of new solutions, rather than rushing in to mend and restore the old automatic pilot.

Although dramatherapists are familiar with this process, some, when confronted by someone in great distress, may feel the strong desire to be able instantly to relieve it by 'turning back the clock'. This is a normal human reaction to such a situation, but therapists must be aware that a failure to acknowledge this may block the progress of the therapy: they may find that they have actually also entered into the 'avoidance' of the reality of the pain.

One client I recall had contacted a long list of professionals after losing her family in a tragedy. She had seen each worker once, after which either they or she had terminated the relationship, increasing her sense of isolation. During her first session with me I told her that, however much I wished I could, I was not able to bring her family back: I had no magic powers, but I was prepared to be there for her. She then admitted that what she had been trying to get the previous professionals to do was to make things as they were before, although logically she knew that that was not possible. She was frightened by how she was thinking and feeling, and needed to find out that people in similar situations also experienced similar feelings of anger, anxiety, panic and desperation. (It is important to note here that during the process of normalisation *similarity* should be acknowledged rather than *sameness*: do not say 'Mrs X felt exactly the same' or 'I know how you feel'; remember and respect the individual's uniqueness.)

One common symptom of PTSD is a needless fear of madness, a feeling of being 'on the edge'. This may also add to the sense of isolation, as onlookers fear being touched by such emotion.

The therapist should remember that these feelings constitute a normal response to an abnormal situation, and that, despite their saying this, feelings of panic, being lost, bewilderment and fear can set in. The sufferer may feel like their world has come to an end but things do still move on: consider a river – it appears to be in the same place, yet the water is ever shifting, journeying onwards.

The following extract from *Duncton Found* (Horwood 1990) shows how story can be used to explore such issues.

> But the wood had opened out alluringly and he had gone on until it had suddenly seemed to darken with the approach of evening. His natural fear of the unknown caught up with him and he had turned to run quickly back to more familiar surroundings which, to his consternation, he had not found... he had tried to keep calm but was failing miserably. It was then, as panic began to overcome him, that from behind and from nowhere, it seemed, an alarming mole appeared.

> Beechen reared up in a not unimpressive stance of self-defence, but one in which he could not seem to prevent his back paws shaking, as the mole raised a paw of greeting...

> '...Forget you are lost. Let your body remind you what your mind has forgotten: *you* can never be lost, since *you* are *here*. Look at your paw! Here. Look at the mark it makes in the dust. Here. Hear your nervous breathing. Evidently here! So *you* are not lost.'

> Beechen pondered this, relaxed, and eventually said doubtfully, 'But I don't know where I am...'

May Weed responds:

> 'Don't say, "I don't know where I am" but "I don't know where this place is". See? Understand? Appreciate?'

> 'Sort of,' said Beechen, who sort of did. Certainly he felt less panic-stricken that he had and, now he saw that the problem was not himself but the place, it was easier to keep calm.

This part of the story, as in the whole book, is rich in metaphor: a group may concentrate on the part that resonates for them. The story acknowledges how the lost mole feels, and listeners may identify with this and share their feelings, but also incorporated in this story is the sense of grounding the other mole is able to give. So in the end Beechen realises that *he* is all right: it is the place that is unfamiliar.

A workshop using this story could be structured in the following way:

Text	Extract from *Duncton Found*
Focus	The normality of fear when faced with the unfamiliar
Length	One and a half hours
Exploratory mode	Primarily drama
Paint	Image of feeling lost Image of finding oneself
Share	Hang up paintings in order, put pieces of paper with words evoked next to painting
Distribute	Copies of text
Read	Extract from *Duncton Found*
Share	Images and ideas evoked by story
Dramatize	In pairs or groups of four each person selects roles to play. Each person selects key words or phrases. Props or long coloured silks* may be available. Scenes are enacted spontaneously and can be played through twice with roles changed or swapped as desired by players.
Share	Dramas in main group without prior discussion.
Discuss	In original sub-group for about five minutes the dramas and any changes you would have liked; difficulties; revelations. In the large group share personal impressions, things that resonated or connections that were made. Consider what has taken place.
In silence	Sit back to back in pairs. Become aware of where you are in the room: how your body feels supported where it touches other surfaces; what the surfaces feel like, and so on. Spend two minutes doing this. When you feel ready, slowly turn to face your partner. Acknowledge them and then acknowledge the others in the room. Prepare to leave as yourself.

---

*   I have found a selection of silks (1x2m) in different colours to be very useful props, as they stimulate the imagination and encourage experimentation with roles. Often, participants will spontaneously pick them up and wrap or drape them around themselves or each other, or will create scenery or pictures by folding or sculpting them into various shapes. The fabric itself is tactile and lends itself to the reflection of light.

Further reading

Dyregrov, A. (1991) *Grief in Children: A Handbook for Adults*. London: Jessica Kingsley Publishers.

Gersie, A. and King, N. (199) *Storymaking in Education and Therapy*. London: Jessica Kingsley Publishers.

CHAPTER 3

Training and Preparation in the Reduction of Risk of PTSD
The Establishment of Group Cohesiveness

> One must know in a crucial situation when to speak and when to be silent, when to act and when to refrain. Action and non-action in these circumstances become identical instead of being contradictory.
>
> *Ghandi 1946*

Training and preparation of workers involved in trauma

The Armed Forces have long recognised the importance of thorough training, to the extent that an individual can carry out his or her task automatically when under adverse and sometimes life-threatening conditions. The effectiveness of this preparation was tested out in the Falklands war: the individuals with less training had a greater incidence of breakdown, and were presumably at greater risk, than those whose more thorough training gave them the ability to work cohesively and receive support from one another. Five hundred Falklands soldiers are reported by British Services as requiring treatment for Post Traumatic Stress (Royal Naval Hospital, Haslar, personal communication). It has become apparent that an important factor in reducing serious stress was group cohesiveness – the concept of 'buddies'. This fosters the ability to put others first and to look out for one another, and while it may also mean that any loss of a member will be sorely felt, a supportive group may provide more opportunities to share feelings.

Thorough training instils a sense of being able to cope, which is vital for workers dealing with trauma. It should also ensure good communications, which is shown to reduce stress.

Every authority or other agency providing such support should have an emergency plan that key staff know and practise, and which is regularly reviewed and updated to reflect the latest knowledge and practice in each speciality involved (e.g. addressing changes in emergency equipment or casualty management). Large gatherings, where there is the possiblity of injury (e.g. carnivals, festivals), and possible hazards specific to the area (e.g. mines, chemical plants, radiation risks) should also be referred to by the plan, with provisional arrangements for the management of such a disaster rehearsed in mock emergency exercises.

Brief guidance such as the following list may also help staff:

- Remember your limitations.
- Disseminate information accurately.
- Be aware of other resources available to help.
- Have definite policies and procedures as to who goes where.
- Be clear and concise in any instructions or delegation.
- Warn against the spreading of rumours or the acting on them.
- Encourage the discharge of feelings away from the immediate scene.
- Be aware that the other members of the team also feel stress.
- Review and update your information at frequent intervals.
- Remember that the management of crisis needs skilled personnel.
- Do not wait until it is too late. Try to be aware of staff under excessive stress.

In the Health Service, much emergency planning does not cover the problem of traumatised staff (Wright 1986), although it is known to account for some sickness and even premature cessation of employment (Cherniss 1980).

There are four particular areas that need attention during training:

1. Group support/cooperation

2. Effective communication

3. Recognition of stages of stress reaction

4. Leadership skills.

Group support/cooperation

The dramatherapist has special skills to offer in groupwork and is able to use these either to assist in the building of a cohesive group or in a 'trouble shooting role', when for some reason the group dynamics have deteriorated, leading, among other things, to a break-down in communication. The dramatherapist may begin by using various practical exercises to assess areas of difficulty, for example, sculpts.

I often use directed sculpts to give me an indication of where people are at that moment. People work non-verbally in pairs, and I may ask one to place his or her partner into a statue shape to represent the sculptor's feelings at that time. They then use a simple title or statement for their sculpt, and the group has the opportunity to view the exhibition. The statues are then encouraged to emerge from the 'wax' and return to themselves, and the roles of sculpt and sculptor are swapped so that all the members of the group have the opportunity to participate and represent how they are feeling. As the dramatherapist, I am given an early indication of how the group works together: are they willing to use this medium? Do they show sensitivity to one another? Are there particular feelings emerging in a pattern, such as anger, anxiety, sadness, denial, hostility, excitabil-ity? Is a sense of caring and support for one another apparent?

The dramatherapist may then use a form of group sculpt in which the group may be asked for suggestions (thus engaging them in sharing ideas and listening to each other) as to what the sculpt could be. One group I worked with had poor dynamics, and much energy was being used up in an unacknowledged power struggle between three of its ten members. They chose to represent a river bank and murky river. The three vying for power all placed themselves on the bank. One was on a stone; two members sat close together on the bank; another sat on the bank with her back to the leaders, looking away from the river; one was a bird surveying the scene; a quiet member of the group described himself as a rainbow-coloured fish, whose colours were hidden by all the pollution in the river. Two others were paddling and unable to get up the slippery bank. It seemed appropriate to let the tableaux come to life, so that individuals could experience the position and role in which they had placed themselves in relation to the rest of the group and also experience what it felt like to move from that position or to help someone else. Those struggling for leadership did so more openly and perhaps became more aware of their destructiveness.

As the dramatherapist, I made no attempt to interpret to the group the significance of what had been portrayed during the sharing of each individual's feelings: when working with metaphor it is important to stay within the metaphor and the unconscious processes, rather than bring in the cognitive and rationalise or sublimate feelings (Watzlawick 1978). I feel that my interpretation would be just that – mine, containing *my* experiences and perceptions and possibly blocking the group members' assimilation of the experience. Metaphor is something that the individual may take away to mull over and use or add to as needed. It is an effective way of working in relation to group dynamics: as it is less threatening than some verbal work, there is less chance to rationalise 'correct' responses beforehand (Shuttleworth 1990). All the group members have an opportunity to express how they feel in relation to the group without being intimidated. They are also able to experiment with different actions/reactions in a safe environment.

The dramatherapist is able to use her knowledge of group dynamics to assist in forming a cohesive team. The importance of functioning as a team has been realised for some time in the Emergency Services (Murphy 1987), and is often fostered by encouraging people to join various sporting activities: although these are often competitive in nature, there is cooperation within the team. One of the features of dramatherapy with a group is that it engages the members in a form of corporate action from the start of a session. Often the group may not be aware that this has begun. Recently I was working with a group of student nurses in a workshop which was expected to give them an insight into PTSD and preventative measures. I was aiming to show them the part peer support and cooperation plays. The following describes the introductory phase of the session:

Structure/activity	Rationale
1. 'Make an imaginary box around you. Explore the boundaries of this box; do not make eye contact with any one else. Walk around the room with your box. Find a space you feel happy/safe in. This is your space to return to at any time in the session that you feel the need.'	Action in group started. The safe space container is always used in any session, as the dramatherapist can never predict what emotions may emerge during any session. This method also contrasts isolation with group.
2. 'Leave your box. Still non-verbally make eye contact with others as you move around the room. As quickly and safely as possible make physical contact with everyone in the room.' The dramatherapist calls together various groups, e.g., brown hair, blue trousers, or other suggestions made by group members.	Barriers broken. Physical contact is made in a non-threatening manner. Laughter. Reflections of various social groupings/experiences of being outside main group. Group members become involved with direction.
3. 'Form a circle. Pass an imaginary ball to one another. The size, type and weight of ball can be changed at the instruction of whoever has possession.' A time limit is imposed by the dramatherapist, saying 'two more throws'.	Cooperation/concentration. Can be used for name learning in unfamiliar group. Engaging of imagination.
4. The group is asked to get into pairs and for one to sculpt his or her partner into a position reflecting 'here and now' feelings. Other sculptors tour the exhibition. Waxworks are instructed to feel the wax melting in the warmth of the sun, and emerge as themselves. Roles are swapped.	The dramatherapist can assess the current mood and feelings of the group. Sub-groups can work in a more intimate cooperative way if they wish. Introduction into importance of de-roling.

5. The group forms back into a circle to discuss and reflect on what has taken place during warm-up, before moving on to the developmental phase.

The dramatherapist can assess what is going on for people and relevance of development phase, showing sensitivity.

The group members asked questions about methods used in forming and strengthening existing groups, to try and lessen the risk of members developing PTSD. This particular group consisted of twelve third-year students who shared an interest in emergency care. One member said she could see the advantages, but how could people be encouraged to work together? I was then able to work through what they had just experienced and explain the aim. Some were surprised that they had been actually doing what they had come to learn about. The developmental phase went on to involve an exercise in which one sub-group used materials to build a structure in which to live, and devised three hidden rules for admission to this sanctuary that the other sub-group had to guess in order to be accepted. The amount of help that was offered to one another was open to negotiation. During the closure phase partners sat back to back, shut their eyes and imagined a video replay of what had taken place, pausing at some things to reflect and, when it came to the end, opening their eyes, stretching, acknowledging others in the room and coming back to the present. (De-roling is a vital part of the closure process, and is particularly useful to learn for future sessions dealing with PTSD). Finally, the circle re-formed and all the members were given the opportunity to state something they wished to take away and to 'throw into the centre' anything they wished to leave behind.

The level of activity undertaken when working on forming or strengthening a group is tailored by the dramatherapist according to the specific group. I often find it more useful to work in an abstract way, rather than just relating it to PTSD, as the skills learnt and experiences gained can be applied by the individual in a variety of settings and life situations, leading to a more integrated mode of living. It is, however, important when designing a training programme to look at the why? when? how? who? what? and where? so that a structured approach with clarity of aim is followed.

Effective communication

As has already been mentioned, in any emergency situation effective communication is vital. If we wait until a crisis to test communication skills, we are doing little to lessen the incidence of factors contributing to PTSD. Dramatherapy is an effective medium for increasing awareness of communication at all levels. This encompasses both verbal and non-verbal communication.

In a training session looking at the use of voice, different tones of speech would be experimented with: soft, loud, dull, monotone inflicted, aggressive, assertive, nervous and so on. This is accompanied by exercises involving a variety of body postures and facial expressions. It seems to me that, although theoretically it is accepted that voice and stance play an important part in the effective handling of any situation, staff are not always afforded the opportunity to try this out in a safe environment, instead having to learn by trial and error.

A dramatherapy workshop that I have used with staff in initial training runs in the following way:

Group details

Second workshop. Group of ten members, four females, six males. Theme: 'Effective communication/getting what you asked for!' The group began the session with, as before, identifying a safe space to return to if required.

Warm-up

1. Members are asked to walk briskly around the room.
2. They are then asked to walk round in the following guises: someone who is angry; someone who is frightened; someone who is drunk; someone who is happy; someone who is down and out; someone who is élite. This list can be, and was, added to by members of the group. They are asked to greet one another when taking on these various guises – this part of session can last between five to ten minutes, depending on how the members of the group respond. The group members are then asked to decide which guise they wish to continue to portray and, this time

with a mixture of people, again to mill around the room greeting one another as appropriate for their character.

3. The group then come together in a circle to reflect on the past exercise, and any comments they wish to make about how it felt taking on various stances. This warm-up has taken up approximately the first fifteen minutes of the session and we now move into the developmental phase.

Developmental phase

4. Members are asked to find a place in which to sit or be comfortable by themselves. They are invited to close their eyes and think of something or someone that makes them angry. They are asked to think about what ways they move their body or behave to express that anger. They are then told to move around the room or to do what they need to do to re-enact this anger. (Sometimes an individual may wish to just sit, because this is the way he or she deals with anger.) The group spend about three minutes in this activity. (They have been reminded at the beginning of the session of the group rules safeguarding themselves and others: they must cause no physical harm or damage to furnishings.)

5. They are then asked to pause and think about what the person or thing that invokes the anger does in return. Again they are instructed to act this. Again, they spend about three minutes in this activity.

6. They are then asked to act what they do in response to this.

7. They are then asked to go back to the place in which they first sat and consider what has taken place for them. When they are ready, they are asked to find partners to share their experiences with.

8. They then come back into the main group and reflect and share as they feel necessary. The purpose of this and the previous exercise is to show how we move our bodies and how we respond physically to how we feel internally.

    There is now a break in the session when coffee or other refreshments are taken, and there is opportunity for free discussion. I also use this part of the session for people to ask questions about the modes of working and other situations where it could be applied. It is usually beneficial to give an example which has proved helpful in treatment. This time also gives the opportunity to emphasise how carefully work of this nature must be undertaken, and that it cannot just be applied by an unskilled facilitator to see what may come about. This may lead to a discussion on ethics. This part of the session is again about communication on a different level – probably the level we are all more used to – so it serves the purpose of bringing the group back to the 'here and now' and the security of something that they are familiar with. This part of the session is limited but lasts between fifteen and twenty minutes – if no time limit is imposed and the session is simply allowed to go on, the lack of structure could be used as a means of avoiding the work to be done in the next part of the session.

9. The group is divided into two halves. The dramatherapist takes one half to the side and instructs them that they are to be various types of shop-keepers. It is near closing time, and they have just cashed up the till and do not wish to sell anything else. They are trying to close on time to get to an important engagement. The other half of the group are instructed that it is nearly closing time and it is a matter of extreme urgency that they get a product from the shop. They are advised that they must make as reasonable a case as possible to gain what they wish. They are made aware of what each person is selling. The exercise has a time limit of three minutes, and they are reminded when they only have one minute left to get what they desire.

10. This exercise takes place again, this time with the roles reversed.

11. Back in the group people are encouraged to identify their difficulties and frustrations with this exercise. Some people find it difficult to say no; others become angry or hurt if they do not get what they wish; some become frustrated; some may become aggressive and raise their voices when not getting their own way; and some may have experienced

an enjoyment of the feeling of power of being able to reject others. It is helpful to be able to discuss these issues in a group and to receive peer support and acceptance, or censure, of different behaviours. It may be that one person's reactions are related to past experiences and it may be appropriate for the dramatherapist to then facilitate exploration of this during the rest of the session. In this particular session one of the women found it particularly difficult to be assertive and to say no, and because of this she eventually became so angry that she became aggressive in her approach to others. She was able to relate this to earlier life, when she had always been corrected by her mother for behaving in an unladylike way when she did not agree with what was happening and challenged things. She said that she felt she had developed a lot of self-control but would get to the point where she would just explode, and this issue was worked on within the group during this session and later sessions. In this individual's work it was important that she could be assertive, but an aggressive form of communication would have been detrimental. Within this session she was helped by creating a scene of her choosing that she had previously experienced, when she had become aggressive rather than assertive. This was an incident where she felt that the equipment she was using would not stand up to requirements. She had complained to her superior that there was a problem, but thought he dismissed it too lightly and, rather than pursue this argument, she had become angry and said, 'I am just wasting my time here: nobody ever takes any notice of me; none of you care about what happens. You'll be sorry when I am proved right.' During the re-enactment she took the same line, at first being very controlled, despite being brushed aside by the person playing her superior, but then suddenly losing her self-control and in so doing losing the argument. Various members of the group 'doubled', that is, took her place standing alongside her, and responded in what they thought may be a more helpful way. She was also advised to be aware of her body posture and breathing, and she tried out this new approach and said she felt better and more in control. The group also went on to look at various problem-solving techniques, such as brain-storming, goal setting, and target setting, which would have enabled her to have a clear aim at the outset.

The closure phase

12. The group were asked to sit in pairs back to back and close their eyes. They were asked to be aware of any areas of tension within their body and to wriggle or shrug these off, still keeping contact with their partner's back. They were asked to be aware of any feeling of anger, sadness or fear, and so on, that they had with them and wished to leave behind. They were asked to make an imaginary pile of this feeling beside them, and then in their mind's eye to imagine striking a match, feeling the warmth from it and setting fire to their pile. They would imagine watching the flames as they leapt high and then gradually died away, leaving a pile of white dust and then seeing a gust of wind take the dust and blow it away. They were then asked to stretch out, open their eyes, acknowledge their partner and then make eye contact with the others in the room and, when they were ready, to move away as themselves, as individuals.

This workshop concentrated on communication in training staff. Its purpose was to make people more aware of the effects of body language and stances, non-verbal communication as well as verbal. As well as being a basis for preventative work in the treatment of PTSD, this type of workshop is useful in enhancing communication techniques for both individuals and organisations. This can be tailored towards purely emergency-work situations but, if we are to take a holistic approach, these skills need to be applied in everyday living, to strengthen team work in all situations, and not just brought out during a critical incident, where there would not have been many previous opportunities to practise them to any great extent.

Recognition and management of stages of stress reaction and the role of leadership

If trainees have attended earlier dramatherapy workshops, they will have become familiar with some of the methods used. It is helpful always to give some indication of the intent of the session and its structure, and to remind the group of definite boundaries regarding space and time. The facilitator will also have in mind the purpose for which she has been asked to run the workshop; it is important that the dramatherapist brings a sense of purpose and order as well as sensitivity into the group, so that trust develops. Participants are then able to follow clearly-given instructions to carry out a sequence of tasks, without the therapist making the whys and wherefores explicit. The task loses a great deal of potency if this happens, as the participant then aims to work in accordance with these stated reasons and anticipates a certain outcome (Gersie and King 1990).

Staff in the emergency services are used to very realistic simulations of trauma and major incidents, and such exercises can cause as much distress as 'live' situations for some workers. Currently, several regions are looking at incorporating psychological aspects into their major incident plans. In structured interviews, some emergency staff identified feelings of emotional distress, and two reported experiencing flashbacks when taking part in a simulated event. It was a pity that no attention had been given to these aspects in training, as it would have had some bearing on the handling of a real situation, and could have been an opportunity for an educational element on PTSD. Of some considerable concern to me as a dramatherapist is that no attention to de-roling is given following these often intensive exercises (Langley 1983). This means some individuals may carry the negative feeling associated with the exercise for some time and be unaware of from where the emotional state has arisen. The person may experience feelings of depression, guilt, anxiety, uselessness, anger or confusion, in fact any of the emotions that may be experienced following a real incident. It would not be practicable to have a dramatherapist present to assist with de-roling every time role-play is used, but those trainers that use it should teach their trainees practicable ways of de-roling (Sue Jennings' book *Creative Drama in Group Work* (1986) describes some useful de-roling exercises). Once individuals have learnt this, the responsibility ultimately lies with them to carry it out, and it is a useful personal skill to have. I have taught it to people in the ambulance service, to the police and to others working with trauma, and on evaluating its usefulness, everyone has found it of benefit when having difficulty switching off or winding down following particular incidents. Some had also passed on their skill to colleagues.

The dramatherapist has special skills in group work which enable her to contribute or set up specific incidents for training purposes. These incidents may be specified by the institution, or suggested or identified as a training need by the group itself. In such a situation I would be using my clinical knowledge to assess accuracy of procedures, approach, methods, and so on, but I would also be assessing factors such as teamwork, leadership skills, co-operation, communication, the ability to cope under stress, areas of difficulty and dissension and their point of origin, where the focus was and how issues are resolved within the group dynamic. I would be observing individuals when they speak, as well as the words they use. Where is the emphasis? What volume, pitch, tone, and range are used? Is there eye contact? Do they recognise and use space and stance? Are there particular areas of difficulty that require working on, in order to get the optimum from the team in crisis? For example, in one such session it became clear that Mike[*] would become aggressive when requesting help from Joe: his tone of voice would become gruff, there was no eye contact. Joe would respond by sauntering over, but when there, fiddle with his hands in a nervous manner, talk almost inaudibly, and invariably became all fingers and thumbs when carrying out a procedure. This was remarked upon by another member of the group during the feedback session, who said, 'I noticed how you behaved and it reminded me of how I used to feel when I had to help my dad.' Joe said that was just how he experienced it and that he resented Mike for making him feel that way, when they were meant to be on equal footing professionally. Mike responded that he was irritated by Joe's lack of hurry and fiddling around when on the job. It reminded him of his younger brother. This was clearly a case of counter-transference that was interfering both with the job·in hand and with the functioning of the team. The matter was resolved by the group over several sessions, but initially I asked them to do a cameo re-enactment of what had taken place, this time asking Mike to soften his voice slightly and to make eye contact with Joe, so he was then able to notice Joe's response. Joe felt more at ease and was not clumsy with the procedure. Thus, though more work was needed on this

*   Not their real names

matter, emotional first-aid was applied from this initial insight: the two could be relied on to function in a crisis and to support one another, and the group could also understand the dynamic, be more supportive, and explore transference issues and how they related to them. In another training session, it may just have been noted that the two did not work well together, or that Joe was not adept at carrying out the task, or that Mike lacked leadership qualities. Instead, this session became a point of growth and strengthening of group bonds, which we have already identified as being so important in the risk reduction of PTSD.

Recognising Stress Reactions

Stress can be a useful precursor to the development of new ideas and creativity. It can cause one to be provoked into action to surmount a difficulty or face a challenge. Individuals respond to stress in different ways and each person has a limit to what they can tolerate before experiencing crisis.

The following are common causes of crisis:

- Lack of information
- Lack of support
- Lack of options.

When someone is failing to cope with stress some of the following behaviours may become apparent:

- Irritability and outbursts of anger, and a tendency to focus this in an unjustified manner.
- Lack of flexibility. The person clings rigidly to what is known and becomes very resistant to any alternative solutions to a problem.
- Dissociative states. The person fails to respond. An example of this is an emergency worker who 'freezes' when requested or expected to perform life-saving duties when called to an incident. Normally, however distressing the scene encountered, the person continues to carry out the procedures he is trained to do – in this instance, however, the 'auto-pilot' malfunctions.

- Isolation. The person can begin to feel isolated and this may result in her pushing away those who can give support. This may increase her sense of being alone and, in its extremes, lead to feelings of persecution.

- Avoidance. In an attempt to gain a sense of stability the person may begin to avoid the situations that he finds stressful. This could lead to an increase in absenteeism in workers in difficult or stressful occupations.

- Over-involvement. The person may deny any problem and become over-involved in her work activities, convincing herself that she is the only one who can provide the answers. An example of this would be the emergency nurse who ceases to work in a team manner and becomes hyper-critical of others. In the end, due to lack of rest, refreshment and sharing, she becomes ineffective and loses her focus and ability to prioritise their work. She may complain that she no longer understands her role.

Leadership

In a critical situation, perhaps following a traumatic incident, it is important that leaders are aware of some of the behavioural signs of difficulty in coping. The model of crisis (Kfir 1989) is a simple one, and addressing it swiftly can go a long way towards preventing chronic stress. A good leader should provide the following to address this model:

- *Information.* The leader should be able to communicate with clarity and ensure that information is being circulated in its entirety. Rumours and speculation will lead to confusion and add to a stressful situation.

- *Support.* This should be readily available from both the leader and peers. As well as support being provided through supervision, a supportive atmosphere should be nurtured in all areas. This provides a firm base and will help people to remain steady in a crisis. If this atmosphere is present from the start, it will be less difficult for the individual under stress to be offered and to accept help.

- *Options.* A good leader should be able to step back from the immediate situation in order to be able to explore other view points and identify alternative solutions. Creativity is useful in addition to the ability to draw on previous experiences.

The person providing leadership has to be aware of team dynamics and even when under pressure maintain good listening skills and a sense of direction. An ability to utilise the whole team's skills and strengths helps both in maintaining and increasing cohesiveness and in giving a sense of purpose and direction whilst working towards the resolution of the situation.

The dramatherapist should be aware of the behaviour that may occur as a result of working in a stressful situation and of the importance of identifying and developing leadership skills in training workshops. She should also be able to provide information, support and options.

CHAPTER 4

Debriefing

All indescribable then, but still the urge to depict, descry, point
out, picture, prepare. The deep darkness had to be spoken of,
touched beyond reach of stars, entered without indications.

Elizabeth Jennings
John of the Cross

Much attention is given to technical debriefs, but recent work I have
carried out shows that little time is given to emotional debriefing –
the listening to and validating of others' experiences. One of the
problems seems to be the reluctance to disclose difficulties to line
managers – it was identified in my work with people in the emergency services that the closest source of support was often peers.
However, many felt they lacked skills to do much emotional debriefing and as a result expressed an interest and a willingness to learn.
They identified a wish to know more about what was normal and
what required more specialist help. They thought it would be useful
to have someone outside the direct service to assist with the debrief,
providing they were professionally competent. One common problem was felt to be the embarrassment of attending a debrief – this has
been resolved in some areas (the Metropolitan Police and some
Accident and Emergency departments) by making the first debrief
compulsory, so that those requiring further help have a point of
contact.

To be given the space to relate one's story is a very important need,
which must be fulfilled to enable the person to continue on his
journey through life. This opportunity is one which does not often
exist in our culture where storytelling has increasingly become a
rarity. I can remember an incident in which one diver had rescued
another and, as a result, suffered from some neurological problems.

He had been receiving medication from the Psychiatric Department because of his aggressive outbursts. I had been advised to not have contact with him as he did not like women. However, one day he presented at clinic when it had been cancelled. I sat with him and he began, at first awkwardly, then with more certainty, to recount his story of the incident: apparently, he had not done this before, and found it a cathartic experience. Of his own volition, and with minimum intervention, he had been freed from his 'stuckness'. He no longer takes psychotropic medication, is very involved in various charitable exploits and, in his words, 'I have got my life together again'. It may be that debriefing at the time of the traumatic event would have saved the Health Service considerable expense, and the man and his family a lot of pain and destruction.

At the initial debrief people are often exhausted and so a prolonged session is not usually helpful. The dramatherapist can assist in the expression of a wide variety of feelings – working with any pressing issues and noting others that may require further work in later sessions. If she is not known to the group the key issue is to build up an atmosphere of trust and acceptance: it is important to be available but not to push during this stage. It is an opportunity to let people know what to expect when and if they experience Post Traumatic stress, and to make it clear that it is a normal response to an abnormal event. This is very important, as the person then realises that what they experience does not mean they are 'going mad' and that further help is available if required.

After the immediate close-to-scene- and-time-of-incident debrief, a further debrief – preferably the following day when people have rested – can take place. Feelings such as 'I should have handled this differently', 'I wish I had said something else' or guilt, anger and grief may be apparent.

The dramatherapist will explore this as circumstances dictate, always having in mind the needs and state of the group. If a session was handled badly, there is a risk of further traumatizing rather than debriefing (Wright 1986). In the event of being called to a situation and not having time to go into complex plans, I ask myself the why, what, when, where, who and how? This maintains my sense of direction and gives me a sense of structure in what may appear to be chaos.

In further debriefing sessions I have used the following ways of working.

Re-enactment

This involves a re-creation of the incident and an exploration of areas of distress, confusion, anger, helplessness and so on, as well as an exploration of things that went well, helped or gave a sense of control. It may be that some group members' interpretations vary. This can be explored.

Empty chair work

It may be that a person feels that they needed to say something to someone who is now lost. An empty chair may be used to represent the missing person and the member encouraged to address that person. Other members in the group may support or join in and the group may then discuss this.

Expression of emotion

In one situation, three group members who attended for a debriefing were extremely angry at what they perceived was the failure of the institution to offer support at a critical time. It seemed we would not be able to move forward until some of those emotions were released. First, I acknowledged their anger and then (reminding them of their responsibility, both for their actions, and towards one another and the space) I asked them what they wanted to do. They decided upon using an empty chair and addressing it as the person they felt anger towards. Other members of the group joined in. This went on for fifteen minutes, in which there was a considerable release of tension and much shouting which gave way to tears. The group was then able to discuss what was going on, whether it was justifiable to feel that way and what they were going to do. Two of the original three were able to identify that some of their anger was due to reawakened feelings from the past and finding themselves in a similar situation. After the release they were calmer and looked at various ways of getting their feelings across to the management of what the failings of the system had meant. They spontaneously role-played this to rehearse and gain some insight into possible reactions.

De-roling was carried out in the form of shrugging off unhelpful feelings and imagining watching them burn, leaving a pile of dust to be blown away by the wind (some time was spent on this, after a session in which much high emotion had been expressed). I then made sure that people felt all right to leave.

Metaphor

If I am offered a metaphor during debriefing I may stay with it for a while. For example, one person spoke of feeling as if he was walking through thick treacle, with more weight being added to his boots all the time and the light being blocked out. I later referred to the treacle and weight, and he responded that he was having difficulty getting all the treacle off and the weight was still quite heavy, but he was no longer sinking and could see some light.

As the dramatherapist facilitating the debrief it is my intention to look at the *moment* – the 'here and now' of emotions and cognitions, not just the feelings and thoughts occurring at the time of the incident.

Tables 4.1 and 4.2 describe Critical Incident Stress Debriefing for staff, which provides a solid framework for the stress and distress associated with the incident. The adoption of these procedures can significantly reduce worker stress and burnout. In the clinical area in which I work staff are introduced to these procedures during their induction and know that they are to be implemented in the instance of a critical incident. This means that they are not faced with something unknown should they have to deal with such a case, and that they are able to use a familiar structure to provide a sense of stability in what may be chaos.

Table 4.1 illustrates the sequence of events. Stage 1, *defusing*, focuses on the cognitive elements and the exchange of information. Stage 2, *demobilising*, provides a structured ending to the span of duty. This should last a maximum of fifteen minutes and its focus is again more on cognitive functioning than emotional ventilation. Further help to facilitate the emotional response is given during debriefing – the aim of demobilisation is to achieve a sense of stability before the session closes. Stage 3, *debriefing*, then takes place as described in Table 4.2. This model of debriefing can be used with anyone who has witnessed or been involved in trauma. It seems that some people who are referred for treatment with a diagnosis of PTSD can respond favourably to debriefing many years after the event and require little other treatment (however, in such cases the debriefing is spread over several sessions).

Table 4.1: Assisting staff following trauma
Stage 1 *Defusing*: (Whole team present)   Developing listening skills   Giving information and reassurance
Normalisation – A normal response to an abnormal occurrence
Stage 2 *Demobilising*: Short duration (all attend).   Exchanging of critical information.   Receiving positive feedback   Providing reassurance.   Providing contact numbers, Helpline numbers, etc.
This marks the end of acute phase
Stage 3 *Debriefing*: This must be carried out by an experienced, skilled debriefer, preferably with knowledge of the set up, but who is separate from incident, and who is prepared to facilitate strong emotions in a safe and confidential setting.
Debriefers need to be aware of their own process!!
(Adapted from Wright 1993).

Debriefing the debriefers

It is important to remember when working with those who are very distressed and when listening to their anguish that the debriefer is also human and has no magical power that exempts him or her from the effect of being in close contact with the anguish of others. The expression of emotion and the revelation of what often are gruesome details may take their toll on the practitioner. A model that is emerging for debriefing is that of a small, close-knit team with adequate

Table 4.2: Debriefing	
24–48 hours after incident	
Phase 1	Introductions, reassurance of confidentiality.
Phase 2	Personal details, Circumstances of incident: role, sight, sound, smell etc.
Phase 3	How did you feel? How are you feeling now? Have you felt like this before?
Phase 4	Changes that have occurred, not only at work, but at home. Has your world picture changed?
Phase 5	Teaching: Stress and its management. Information: Common signs and symptoms.
Emphasise: Normal reaction to abnormal, distressing occurrence	
Phase 6	Re-entry phase. Loose ends gathered. Reassurance, rest and recreation.

skills and experience to support one another in this work. During a period of debriefing, firm arrangements should be made for the debriefers to meet together every two hours for a fifteen-minute break to review performance, difficulties and feedback. This can be a time for the debriefers to give vent to their feelings of frustration and so on, and it provides an opportunity for people to be aware of their colleagues' needs. For a variety of reasons ranging from exhaustion to difficulties at home someone may be in need of more help or of being relieved of some responsibility. At the end of a debrief the team should meet for a lengthier review in which to exchange information and develop further plans.

It is also important that the debriefers take care of themselves in order to care for others. This means adequate rest, breaks and time out from the work. An external person may be best equipped to deal with these organisational matters. I well remember one instant when someone from the secretarial staff quite unobtrusively would produce chairs and cups of tea when she saw the need and also screened out those from the media seeking information through the 'back door'. Her help and quiet support were invaluable.

A word of caution here. As PTSD has become more recognised some professionals of various disciplines have accepted the importance of debriefing and have taken on the role themselves, without having had adequate training or experience. This is of concern on two points: first the risk to themselves, but also the effect this can have on a client. I have seen clients who have said that when they began recounting the story of what they had experienced to an untrained professional, the listener had recoiled, changed the topic or, at the end of the session, said that the person needed to seek help elsewhere. This mirrored the sense of loss the teller had experienced previously. In the words of one woman I worked with: 'I knew it was difficult to bear, and when I looked at her face I felt worse that I had now upset her. I felt desperate. I tried to pretend it was not so bad so she would feel better.'

Allowances of course need to be made for the client's projection, but that was how it seemed to her. As a supervisor I have also worked with supervisees who have brought such instances to supervision.

Even after a debriefing session for themselves, workers may carry something away with them. If someone has been debriefing a rape victim then they may feel anger towards their partner who tries to be sexual towards them. If someone has debriefed those involved in an accident with multiple fatalities they may feel anxious for the safety of their family. Within a close-knit team these feelings can be disclosed and the 'normalness' of them realised. This form of debriefing does not, of course, diminish the need for supervision, which is dealt with in Chapter 8.

Further reading

Mitchell, J.T. (1983) When disaster strikes – the critical incident stress debriefing process. *Journal of Emergency Medical Services.*

CHAPTER 5

Key Concepts in the Treatment of Post Traumatic Stress Disorder

To feel that though I journey on
By stoney paths and rugged ways.
The blessed feet have gone before
And strength is given for weary days.

Anonymous, Hymns and Psalms 421

During my involvement in training a variety of individuals in the treatment of PTSD a number of key concepts have emerged. This chapter describes them. They can be helpful in providing structure to the work, and yet allow for flexibility in meeting the needs of the individual or group.

I would identify seven key concepts:

1. Assurance of confidentiality and trust building.

2. The educational element: anxiety management, what PTSD is.

3. Listening to the whole story: do not assume it has been told before.

4. The paradigm: ritual v risk.

5. Paying tribute: often necessary before a person can continue their journey through life.

6. Moving forward: much energy is wasted by the PTSD sufferer and their families trying to get back to how things were. We can use our experiences to move forward.

7. Responsibility: ultimately the individual must take responsibility for his or her actions.

Assurance of confidentiality and trustbuilding

The person that comes to treatment rarely does so without trepidation. It is important to remember that the person is already traumatised and wary of anything that may add to that. The issue of confidentiality is always made clear at the first session and a written agreement to this effect may be given – if a team is involved in treatment then the boundaries of information sharing and the purpose of it needs to be made clear to the client. If treatment is to be carried out in a group setting the participants must agree to keep what takes place in the group confidential, and it must be ensured that each individual grasps the meaning of any group guidelines that are formulated.

The first session can be used to negotiate the format of treatment and the expectations of both client and therapist. Often the client has lost confidence and expects things to be done to or for them, particularly if treatment of physical injuries has left them feeling depersonalised. It is an opportunity to engage with each other, and it forms the beginning of the therapeutic liaison. The client should feel free to ask about the therapist's level of skill with PTSD, whether she is using dramatherapy or another form of treatment. At this stage I take care not to overwhelm the person or group, although I normally do say that during treatment they may become distressed and find things painful. I stress that any time they want to stop during a session they may do so and we will then look at the reasons for the difficulty. Some clients have told me that when I told them this, and reminded them of it on occasion, they thought it a strange thing to say and they had wondered what to expect. However, during therapy they had remembered it and felt safe and assured that they would not be pushed beyond their endurance. As with psychotherapy for any psychological problem, trust is built up over the sessions and depends to a large extent on the openness and honesty of both therapist and client.

The educational element

It is helpful early on to share with the sufferers a brief description of the signs and symptoms, that are common in PTSD. Some professionals argue that this may increase the person's anxiety or despondency, but I have found it usually elicits expressions of relief such as

'I felt I was going mad – I couldn't understand what was happening to me' or 'I felt so alone, so isolated in this before'.

During the initial assessment, if the client reports somatic symptoms, a description of what happens when one becomes physiologically aroused can do a lot to quell fears that a heart attack is imminent, although, of course, the practitioner should ensure that physical problems have been thoroughly checked. This sharing of information assists in giving a sense of empowerment to the client, who can then take some positive steps to control his or her own body.

The client may already know the definition of PTSD or may have been informed by another professional that this appears to be what he or she is suffering from. It is important that the therapist assesses the level of knowledge that the person has and what his or her understanding of the diagnosis is – there is a danger that the person may have just collected this label or name without really understanding why. On the other hand, the client may not even have been told what is considered to be wrong with them, but just sent for 'therapy'.

If they are to be active participants in their recovery they need to know what factors are being considered. This may be the first opportunity that the sufferer has had to ask questions about the symptoms he has been experiencing, and it is also a good time for the therapist to introduce the fact that ultimately the individual is responsible for his actions and behaviour. The distress the person experiences is very real, but once having been given a label for it, some will use it in a very negative way, for example as an excuse for various maladaptive behaviours such as excessive drinking, violence and irritability towards those close to them. At this stage it is also very helpful, with the client's agreement, to involve significant others, so they may understand some of what they have been witnessing. These significant others may have also become traumatised by this behaviour, even if they were not directly involved in the original incident.

As treatment develops the person may be exposed to anxiety-arousing situations – he may already have marked anxiety responses. It is for this reason that both during and after assessment it is important to teach basic anxiety management skills. This can be done by a simple explanation of how anxiety can affect the body (see Figures 5.1 and 5.2). Many people are relieved to know that the physical symptoms they have experienced are normal, that they are not in imminent danger of a heart attack and that there is nothing seriously wrong with them. (However, if the therapist is at all concerned about a client's physical well-being then they should persuade them to have a full physical check up.) One very effective way of dissipating feelings of panic or tension is slow deep breathing; I encourage people to take a maximum of six deep breaths (Figure 5.2), concentrating on breathing in refreshing, renewing air and breathing out tension. I ask clients to carry this out at various times, not always when they are feeling very tense, and to practise and be aware of the benefits so that it becomes second nature and may be useful during treatment sessions. If patients agree, then it may be helpful for them to enlist significant others in reminding them of this simple exercise whenever they are noted to be getting anxious. It should be emphasised not to breathe in this way too quickly or for too long, or else there is a danger of the person becoming light headed or having pins and needles sensations, which again may be mistaken for anxiety. It may be helpful to give clients written instructions or diagrams as a reminder, as it is sometimes difficult for them to remember what is said between sessions. This may be due to poor concentration (one of the factors of PTSD), or it may be that the person has suffered a head injury (some may have received head injuries during their traumatic incident).

What is anxiety?

Anxiety is normal. People have always used it to help them survive. It helps people by making their bodies work faster and harder if they get into dangerous situations. For instance, if you are crossing a road and notice a car coming rapidly towards you, it is your anxiety which helps you jump out of the way.

By looking at this a bit more closely, we can see what happens when a person gets frightened and anxious. First of all, the person needs to be aware that something is threatening her. When she is aware of this, her body will be able to take some action to prepare her to run away or fight. It does this as shown in Figures 5.1 and 5.2.

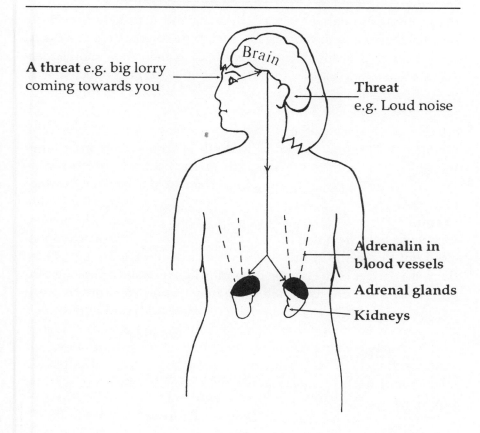

A threat e.g. big lorry coming towards you

Brain

Threat e.g. Loud noise

Adrenalin in blood vessels

Adrenal glands

Kidneys

Figure 5.1: The Anxiety Management Package by Hilary Jupp, RGN, RMN, RNT, ENB

The eyes and ears sense a threat and pass on the information to the brain. The brain tells the adrenal glands on the top of the kidney to release *adrenalin* into the blood vessels, which carry it through the body.

The adrenalin which the adrenalin glands release is passed around the body in the blood stream. When it reaches the heart, lungs, muscles and so on, it makes changes to help you fight or run away, as shown below.

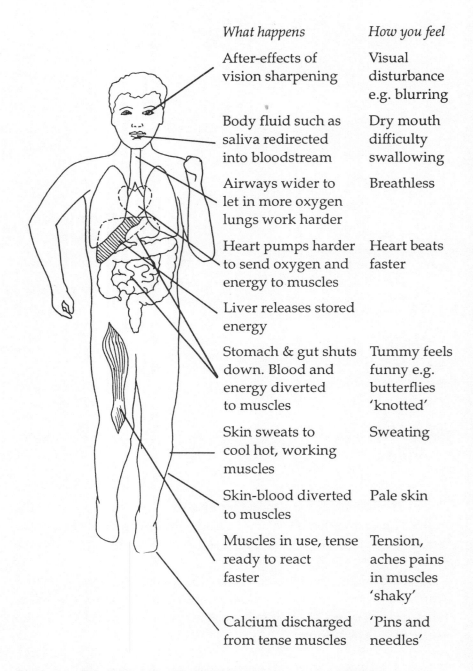

What happens	How you feel
After-effects of vision sharpening	Visual disturbance e.g. blurring
Body fluid such as saliva redirected into bloodstream	Dry mouth difficulty swallowing
Airways wider to let in more oxygen lungs work harder	Breathless
Heart pumps harder to send oxygen and energy to muscles	Heart beats faster
Liver releases stored energy	
Stomach & gut shuts down. Blood and energy diverted to muscles	Tummy feels funny e.g. butterflies 'knotted'
Skin sweats to cool hot, working muscles	Sweating
Skin-blood diverted to muscles	Pale skin
Muscles in use, tense ready to react faster	Tension, aches pains in muscles 'shaky'
Calcium discharged from tense muscles	'Pins and needles'

Figure 5.2: RGN, RMN, RNT, ENB The Anxiety Management Package

As we can see, a lot of different things happen when we are afraid to help us deal with what frightens us – to help us run or fight. However, sometimes we think we are threatened when there is nothing to fight. This makes us feel physically unpleasant because our body, with the help of adrenalin, has made these preparations to fight and there is nothing to use them on. What tends to happen is that we run away and therefore feel better. We then learn that running away makes us feel better and it is more likely that when we next face that particular situation, we run away rather than face it. Figure 5.3 summarises this:

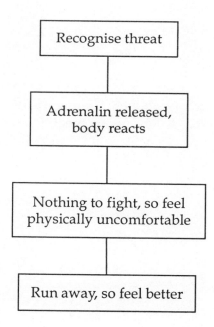

Figure 5.3

If we can't run away or fight then we carry on feeling bad until our adrenalin is used up, which can take quite a while, especially if we say upsetting or useless things to ourselves. For instance, if we feel physically uncomfortable, we tend to say things like: 'This is terrible, I feel awful', 'Will this never go away', 'People will think I'm stupid' and 'I wish I was somewhere else'.

These thoughts are not useful, and may make us feel more frightened – this then releases more adrenalin making us feel physically *more* uncomfortable.

To summarise, anxiety is normal. We all have it to deal with threats. It *will not kill us* because it is there to help us survive. There are three parts to anxiety – physical feelings, running or frightened action, and thoughts.

Important things to remember

1. Anxiety is normal.
2. Anxiety helps us to deal with threats.
3. Unpleasant physical feelings are often due to anxiety.
4. Unhelpful, worrying thoughts may make anxiety worse.
5. Anxiety will *not* kill.

Deep Breathing

Most of the time we aren't aware of our breathing. It's controlled without us even thinking about it. If you ran up a steep hill, however, you would almost certainly notice breathlessness. When you are tense and anxious you may also notice this. Then you may tend to breathe more rapidly and shallowly, using only the top parts of your lungs, like this:

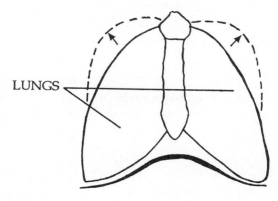

Figure 5.4: Muscle (Diaphragm)

It is useful to be able to stop and take a couple of deep breaths, expanding and using all of your lungs at such times. Actors, for example, often do this before going on stage. Breathing slowly and deeply enables you to take in more oxygen, which your tuned-up body needs.

To do this effectively when you do feel tense or anxious, you need some regular practice, two or three times each day. You'll find it easier if you find somewhere warm, comfortable, quiet and where you will not be disturbed for five minutes. Settle down and make yourself comfortable – either lying or sitting down.

To be able to breathe slowly, deeply and effectively you need to use all of your lungs, not just the top part, but to expand the whole of your chest, including the big muscle at the bottom, the diaphragm.

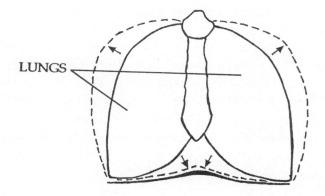

LUNGS

Figure 5.5: Muscle (Diaphragm)

To check that you are doing this effectively, sit or lie down with your hands lightly resting across the lower part of your chest, just slightly above your waistline (if you can find it!), with your fingertips just touching. Take a deep breath in, slowly counting to five, pause for a second, and then breathe out slowly – again counting to five. Pause and then repeat this three more times.

If you are effectively practising deep breathing and expanding the whole of your chest and lungs then your fingertips will move apart when you breathe in, and move together again after you have breathed out. Then sit quietly for another minute or so before carrying on with your daily life.

Regularly practising this exercise will lead you to become aware of shallow, rapid breathing when you are tense or anxious. Practice will enable you to be prepared to use deep breathing to control some of the physical bits of that anxiety 'lump'.

You only need to take four deep breaths each time you practice to get the benefit. Do *not* continue deep breathing for long periods of time.

Listening to the whole story

Perhaps it is my insatiable love of books that makes me firmly believe that every person has a story to tell, and that storytelling is as natural as breathing. However, in late 20th-century Britain its importance has somehow got lost amongst the concepts of a society more based on material values, where if one pauses too long one may lose one's place in the queue.

Part of the treatment for PTSD is to get the sufferer to retell the events as he or she perceives them. In one centre, where a behavioural approach is offered on an intensive group basis, during the third week members are asked to write an account of the incident. This is typed in a draft version, given back to them to check and alter if necessary and then read out by the individual to the group. The group support each other and facilitators work closely with the members. A collage is made and in the fourth week the individuals are recorded on video explaining their collage to a facilitator and responding to questions from the facilitators or the other group members. The recordings are made into individual copies and then the group facilitators and members view them once more and discuss them. The members take their personal copy when they leave. Some choose to show them to significant others.

Some treatment programmes ask the sufferer to make an audio cassette describing the incident during a session and then replay this regularly using relaxation techniques until the anxiety levels subside (Keane and Kalonpek 1982). The principle behind this is that of 'flooding' or desensitisation.

When trust has developed I aim to get sufferers to relate their whole story. Usually they have begun to relate fragments of what happened. They are asked to write an account and share it, or they may initially provide a verbal account that is then written down or put on to a tape. Dramatherapy is used in the further development of this work, and is described in more detail in later chapters.

The telling of the story can be cathartic, frightening, or can reveal the extent of the clients 'stuckness' and inability to recall what happened. In the act of telling, we allow another human being access to our experience of life, our inner world, the journey on which we've been (Gersie and King 1990). As the therapist, before I begin such work I have to be committed to stay with the person on the journey, to let the story flow and not to block it unconsciously because of my own discomfort or distress. When I listen to the story I make few interruptions and use mainly non-verbal encouragement. Long silences often only occur when the client is searching for words to describe the experience. A session in which this work takes place may be lengthy and it is most important to avoid being disturbed. Attention should be made to the closure of the session: that time – at least twenty minutes – is spent checking that the person is back in the here and now and feels all right to leave. The therapist should already be aware of the client's support network and the clients should be aware of whom they can contact between sessions if necessary.

If the person's account has been particularly full of self-blame, the therapist may be tempted to make interventions to make the person look more positively or realistically at their position. At this stage, however, though I would stress the importance of just allowing the person to tell it how it was for them.

The paradigm: ritual versus risk

Dramatherapy may be used to treat people who are locked in almost institutionalised rituals and structures: in this case the therapist is looking to facilitate an increase in risk-taking which may lead to a heightening of physiological arousal, and an increase in levels of energy. Someone experiencing the symptoms of PTSD usually has an exaggerated physiological response, so it is often helpful to provide some ritual within the structure of sessions. This helps to create a safe container – an environment in which to explore the chaos. Some clients create their own ritual, as the following example shows. A session with this particular client would begin:

Therapist: 'How have things been?'

Client: 'Not so bad really.'

Therapist: 'Oh.'

The client would then elaborate on how her week had been. After four of five sessions she commented that she always responded in that way and that she had come to look on it as the 'opening cue' which preceded deeper work, helping her to feel safe. I could have changed my opening question but recognised and respected that she felt comfortable with this and that perhaps it balanced out some of the traumatic things she worked through during the sessions.

When using dramatherapy there is always a warm-up phase before the developmental phase and the closure phase. Sue Jennings (1986) suggests that a quarter of the total session time be spent on the warm-up or preparation, half the session spent on the development of the work and the final quarter spent on the closure, thus enabling individuals to leave as themselves. I support this and feel that such a structure helps to create a feeling of safety, which paradoxically allows for greater exploration and expression of distress. I may sometimes find it necessary, depending on the content of a session, to extend the closure phase to the same length of time as the developmental phase if participants have been re-enacting the particular incident that led to the PTSD. In other words, I aim to create a balance between the risk-taking and the ritual.

Some groups may find that a particular warm-up they have used, such as the creation of a safe-space or visualisation of a special safe room, is helpful and request that this be used in each session. This is good, as it means they are able to state a need and find a way to meet it, thereby increasing their sense of autonomy and responsibility for themselves.

Therapists treating PTSD using an approach other than dramatherapy can also consider the use of ritual by considering such things as the circle, group guidelines and how the group's progression is facilitated in a structured way.

Any reader who feels concerned that to provide such a structure may limit creativity, can be assured that on the contrary, it seems to free individuals of some of their fear and uncertainty and give them room to express and work through their distress.

Paying tribute

Often a person who is suffering from PTSD has been involved in or witnessed an accident where there has been a death (either singular or multiple). He or she may or may not have known the deceased. Within a 'normal' grieving process there is often a reluctance to 'let go', when the bereaved become distressed at any attempt by others to get them to pick up the threads of living. 'How can life go on without —— ?' 'I can't carry on otherwise —— will think I never cared'. This time of adjustment is respected and accepted in most cultures – there seems little anyone can do except wait and be there for those affected (Gersie 1991). It is important to acknowledge that this is part of the journey and not to try to take the clients' feelings and experiences from them, but rather to work with them.

During the course of treatment for PTSD, as long as the therapist is sensitive to cues, it will become clear when the person is ready to work on this area. I think that to push a person on this can be damaging and set back, if not abort, the therapeutic process. It is not possible to prescribe how many sessions should have taken place before the time is right, but a firm therapeutic alliance with an atmosphere of trust ought to pervade. In these times of financial constraints, it may be important to ask oneself whether that is a factor that is encouraging the decision. In my experience, clients will more often than not express a desire to acknowledge the departed. They also often have ideas of how they wish to do this.

Photographic work

A collection of photographs of the deceased may be brought into a session, and the client is encouraged to talk about the person(s), when the photographs were taken, and any particular thoughts or feelings that are aroused. I may then ask the client to select the one that is most special to her (it is important to handle the photographs carefully and with respect). I then talk as if the photo is the person and ask the client if there is anything she needs or wants to say to the person. What emerges may be explored further in that session or later ones. 'Empty chair' work (Jennings 1990) may be used to facilitate further such expression. Time is spent on the closure of the session so that the person is returned to the present and the photograph seen as a token of the deceased.

Revisiting the scene or the grave

Clients may express a desire to visit and possibly leave flowers at the scene of the trauma. As well as paying tribute, this can be a testing of the skills they have developed in managing their anxiety or sense of panic. Sometimes they may wish the therapist to accompany them. It can be a big step on the journey. It can be valuable for others within the family to do the accompanying, as even if they were not affected directly by the incident, significant others do become affected by the PTSD sufferer's symptomatic behaviour. Wishing to make such a visit is a sign that the person is finding his or her way back to independence and self-confidence. It is helpful for the therapist to see the client shortly after the visit to explore what feelings were aroused and assist with the process as necessary.

It may not be possible to revisit the scene of the incident or the grave for a variety of reasons. If this is the case, dramatherapy can be used to re-create a scene that is decided upon by the client. He will often do this metaphorically, and it is useful to have a variety of 'props' available – many lengths of coloured cloths (both bright and dark), blankets, boxes, figures, string and so on. I have worked this way with both individuals and groups: groups obviously allow for greater opportunity for sculpting, role reversal and support, but individuals, too, have gradually become accustomed to working in this way during earlier sessions and often surprise me with the intensity of their work. The dramatherapist creates the 'safe container' (Jennings 1987) in which this can happen. It is important, I think, for her to remain external – although facilitative – to the recreation so maintaining a sense of 'holding' for the clients. Again, much attention must be paid to the closure phase and the processing of what may be a powerful experience.

It may be helpful to have candles that can be lit at the culmination of the tribute. The participant(s) may want to say a final few words. They can be asked to recall the session, look into the candle flame and imagine cleansing, healing images; to close their eyes and feel the warmth from the flame, and in their mind's eye see it slowly die down, feel the wax melting and then to finally have a slow stretch and yawn to emerge from the 'wax' as themselves. The therapist must obviously be sensitive to the clients' needs and experiences in the choice of imagery, as flames would not be helpful to someone who had been involved in a fire. In one such case a person made a cave which contained 'treasures' for the deceased, and in another someone created an imaginary box with various hopes inside to give to the dead ones. It is often useful to have a camera handy as some clients express a wish to have a reminder of what they created.

Story-telling and poems

Alida Gersie has written an excellent book, *Storymaking in Bereavement* (1991), which contains many myths and structures that can be used equally well at this stage with people suffering from PTSD. However, the clients may suggest their own favourite story or poem that resonates for them, which perhaps was also known to the deceased. Roethke's *The Abyss* (1975) has often been used, with different verses speaking to different people.

A group may choose to create their own story as a 'tribute', which can be helpful in that it encourages the sharing and growth in confidence. The facilitator can assist by taking notes as the story grows, so there is a record of it should the group want to use it in further sessions. Whichever method is used, the individuals may decide upon enactment, painting or modelling to express their work further.

Readers may understand about paying tribute to those we love but not those who were strangers. Those with a deep faith may think that any other form of tribute is unnecessary (although I have found that the need to do this or not is unrelated to the amount of faith someone has). The reason I see paying tribute as an effective part of the treatment option for PTSD is illustrated by the person who may have become obsessed with finding out everything about the dead, to the extent that they are 'stuck' and have ceased to interact with significant others. She may neglect her own physical as well as emotional needs. Sometimes this obsession is a way of blocking out other painful memories and emotions that she fears will overwhelm her. One woman I worked with said that the thought of having to acknowledge the stranger killed in an accident in which she was involved appalled her, although at the time her thoughts were saturated by this person's death. However, when she was ready she did pay tribute, faced him, and said she felt able to put him on the periphery. She was then able to be free enough to explore her own fears and the thoughts of dying she had had during the accident – she had become ready to move forward from her 'stuckness'.

On a final note here, as a dramatherapist and person working with PTSD, I find certain accounts very sad and haunting – despite my personal faith – particularly when children or babies have died. In such cases I have paid a tribute myself in a variety of ways, such as lighting a candle or using imagery such as a very precious box, delicately wrapped and fastened with special, beautiful ties, safely containing and guarding the person's memories.

Nobody can ever go back

> Through the night of doubt and sorrow
> Onward goes the pilgrim band.
>
> *B.S. Ingemann (1789–1862)*
> ***Through the Night of Doubt and Sorrow (Hymn)***

There are times when I wish I could wave a magic wand and put things back as before – this is magical thinking, the 'if only', and I can often share the clients' heartfelt cries. However, we know that with each day – each minute – that passes we change, and even though that change may be only cellular and unremarkable, combined with many other minute alterations it makes up what we are. In treatment, from the very beginning of the assessment, I introduce the fact that it is not possible for anyone to go back, although it is normal to grieve for what is lost. Very often as treatment progresses, patients pass a remark such as 'I feel I'm nearly back to normal'; however, at a later stage and usually without prompting, they correct their statement with phrases such as 'I feel I've moved forward and can accept the changed me' or 'I'm a different person, I have emerged from this experience with a new me – it's as if I've had to start learning about the new person'.

One person I worked with likened this period of change to the uncertainties of adolescence, and many describe a sense of relief when they have stopped trying to go back, exhausting all their physical and emotional energy in the fruitless quest.

I introduce the metaphor of a journey early on in dramatherapy sessions. It is one which seems to be easily assimilated by clients and which helps the image of moving forward – when their journey gets tough, rather than simply going back to before, they talk of hilly ground, boulders, bog and so on. They provide the descriptions and

I stay with their imagery, perhaps asking what may help them along the path or what they can see further on. Sometimes I may say it is all right to rest a while where they are to gain some strength. The responses I use vary with individuals or groups, as I use sensitivity and listening to discern a way forward. The therapist may act as a guide on the journey, but must keep her eye on the light so that, although she knows the dark, she too does not get lost. A guide is only needed for a limited time over unknown or difficult terrain, before the traveller reclaims independence.

Responsibility

Often, people I have worked with have spoken of the feeling of being disempowered. This may result from the fact that the nature of the injuries sustained has meant there has been a period of time when they have had to rely totally on others for all their bodily needs.

The human spirit may resist this feeling at first, but a combination of necessary physical treatment, re-active depression and loss of confidence may mean the person loses all autonomy. If they then develop PTSD there is a danger that this label may be used to explain all behaviour. The sufferer may develop an alcohol or other drug dependency, or they may be physically violent or reckless with their life or others' lives. Often families bear the brunt of this. It is important that, whilst recognising and offering treatment for PTSD, it is emphasised that ultimately the individual is responsible for his or her actions and choices. This message is also, ideally, conveyed to their significant others. The sufferer may well be distressed during some of the treatment sessions and on anniversaries or other key dates. He can be supported through this distress and it should be acknowledged that it is difficult for him. However, if he aims to move on from where he is, then it is necessary that he does not use the label of PTSD to maintain the *status quo*.

Some people have said that the fact that they have been expected to take responsibility during sessions and make decisions has been the beginning of a sense of control and self-empowerment. The therapist needs to monitor her interactions and take care that, in trying to alleviate suffering, she does not reinforce the original feeling the client has of being disempowered.

Conclusion

These key concepts are helpful but should be applied with flexibility, according to the clients' needs. In the end they should lead to the person facing his or her fear in order to be able to move on.

> 'I'm frightened,' said the youngster not moving at all. The wood was suddenly hushed and awed about them, and the air stilled as the light seemed to tremble and darken.

> 'The best way with fear is to turn your snout towards it and put one paw resolutely in front of another,' said Trufan.

> *(Horwood 1989)*

Further Reading

Assurance of confidentiality and trustbuilding

Bruch, H. (1974) *When Strangers Meet*. Cambridge, Mass.: Harvard University Press.

Listening to the whole story

Gersie, A. and King, N. (1990) *Storymaking in Education and Therapy*. London: Jessica Kingsley Publishers.

The paradigm: ritual versus risk

Jennings, S. (1990) *Dramatherapy with Families, Groups and Individuals*. London: Jessica Kingsley Publishers.

Paying tribute

Grainger, R. (1990) *Drama and Healing: The Roots of Dramatherapy*. London: Jessica Kingsley Publishers.

Kushner, H.S. (1981) *When Bad Things Happen to Good People*. London: Pan.

Lewis, C.S. (1969) *A Grief Observed*. London: Faber and Faber.

Nobody can ever go back

Cox, M. (1988) *Structuring the Therapeutic Process: Compromise with Chaos*. London: Jessica Kingsley Publishers.

CHAPTER 6

The Use of Dramatherapy Groups in the Treatment of PTSD

Oh people you shall not drown in your tears
But tears shall bathe your wounds.
Oh people, you are not weak in your suffering
But strong and brave with knowing.

Cassin 1979 (p.336–7)

Group work has been recognised as playing an important part in the treatment of PTSD since the First World War, when psychotherapists used the process in the treatment of shell shock. Dramatherapy has much to offer the group work process. Very often, people suffering from PTSD have become 'stuck' and unable to integrate their experience into the rest of their lives, and this in turn may have lead to an inability to perform their normal duties properly. This can have a variety of effects, from unreliability in a work situation, including increased absence or the inability to cope effectively with a critical incident (possibly endangering colleagues), to long-term alcohol and social problems. 'One cannot steer a car unless it is moving' (Tournier 1965) – the first move has to come from the individual seeking assistance for the problem.

When looking at 'stuckness' I find it helpful to consider *rites de passage* (Van Gennep 1960) – the form of life transition ritual that accompanies us from birth to tomb, and marks important changes in how we and others perceive us, such as baptism, initiation ceremonies, marriages and funerals, to name just a few. These transitions occur in various guises, regardless of culture or creed. Van Gennep identifies three important changes: separation, transition and re-incorporation. When a major life change occurs, whatever our culture or creed we experience the process of separation (from that which we knew, or an aspect of it). This leads into transition as we adjust to the change: we make new internal maps and boundaries and explore what these changes mean to us. When we have gained an equilibrium we move on to re-incorporation or re-integration, as we are more ready to re-engage with those around us.

Based on this idea, Hellmann (1984) argues that therapy itself can be described as a *rite de passage*. The transition stage is often the stage a client is experiencing when seeking therapy. Clients feel they are in a 'no man's land' and are, to use Turner's (1969) definition, *liminal* people: 'The attributes of liminality or of liminal personae (threshold people) are necessarily ambiguous... Liminal entities are neither here nor there, they are betwixt and between positions assigned and arrayed by law, custom, culture and ceremonial...' This liminal time can be one of learning and change. As a therapist I may accompany clients on this stage of their journey. I can provide a structure within which they can work (the safe container); I and other group members may be able to help an individual identify what she needs to help her move forward; I may be able to provide some information about the signs and symptoms of PTSD and the obstacles encountered to give some light to the travellers. Each member of the group will be affected by what he or she encounters; the therapist cannot divorce herself from the interaction, and once the journey begins there is no returning to things exactly as they were before; therefore, this process is not to be entered into lightly, or if ill-prepared – to do this may be compared with someone taking a group out on a fell walk in winter with only lightweight clothing, trackshoes, no map and no first-aid kit or torch. 'The dramas of other people's lives also belong to our lives and the drama of the group's life is also the drama of Life itself. Whatever the moment of intra-psychic and inter-psychic reality we may be involved in with our clients, it has an existential reality as well' (Jennings 1987). Dramatherapy is about the 'here and now', the moment. In the group we look at past events and possibly reconstruct them; we may explore the 'what ifs?', but we are bringing them to the *now*; we must work with the feelings, emotions, and cognitions the individual and group are experiencing in the present space. It is, I feel, important to keep hold of this concept, as therapy that concentrates solely on past events can interfere with the process of healing, blocking consolidation and reincorporation, and encouraging the group to avoid moving on from their past experiences and exploring and coming to terms with how it is for them in relation to others at the current moment.

Often, clients I have worked with who are suffering from PTSD have described themselves as being in a jungle, a swamp, a dark cave, or an abyss. These metaphors, although desperate, are actually a form of creativity as the individual struggles to make sense of his or her life. This liminality, or wilderness period, can be a time for reflection. Turner (1967) suggests this period is a time when there are moments of clarity and illumination, when there is a possibility of discovering what we do know. Jennings (1987) argues that we need know that it is our own experience of the darkness, the desert, the fear, chaos and wounding, that will enable the client to make use of his or her own experience. I would say that within every group there is a great potential for members assisting one another through the journey. The dramatherapist does well to be sensitive to this fact and to encourage this process, using the dramatic media to further facilitate expression, learning and possibilities. Often the need to explain or interpret arises from our own feelings of anxiety rather than to do with the needs of the group. If the group perceives the therapist as all powerful, the members may feel little need to do anything to bring about change and so not progress to maturity, reincorporation and finally individuation. When beginning to work with a group of adults I emphasise that they are responsible for their own actions and behaviour. This is particularly relevant in the case of PTSD where members may have adopted maladaptive coping mechanisms, including violent or disruptive behaviour, that have been excused because of their mental state. One of the advantages of group therapy is that although the other members of the group are supportive, they will also challenge such behaviour as they have also been there and very often have used the same excuse.

I was able to attend a treatment programme for PTSD at the Royal Naval Hospital, Haslar. The course ran over three weeks and had five people in treatment for PTSD. They had previously been screened for their suitability for the programme, and been able to attend the open group that is held on a one-session-a-week basis to gain some idea of what went on. The cohesion of the group was increased by their being able to share accommodation and the fact that it was held over a concentrated period of time, away from other distractions. The programme was well-structured and behaviourally based. I was particularly interested in the use of creativity within the programme. Members both wrote and told personal accounts of the traumatic incidents that they had experienced, and recounted their life stories: this fits in with the importance given in dramatherapy to storytelling and its therapeutic value (Gersie 1983). The individuals described initial feelings of trepidation at having to recall incidents they had tried to avoid, but also relief at having been able to tell others. They had support from one another. In daily diaries they were able to write of their feelings and concerns, and these were to be read each day by the facilitators – it was up to the participants whether they shared them with anyone else.

In the third week they each made a collage relating to their PTSD, and afterwards they were interviewed and asked to describe aspects of it. This interview was video-taped, and they were each given a copy to take home. In PTSD, communication often becomes a casualty, as there is a sense of isolation and a feeling that no-one else would understand, or, as I have found in my work with the emergency services, a wish to protect others from distress. Each person, however, planned to show their video to significant others. It was noticeable that there was none of the camera-shyness often present when a video is being made as each person was wrapped up in explaining their collage. The staff commented that this was usually the case, although the participants doubted they would have been able to do this early on in the course – as in any group, timing of certain work has to be carefully considered.

There is a strong information and education element of the Haslar course, and this is important as it helps sufferers and their families (who often experience secondary suffering) identify what has been happening and offers practical ways of reducing anxiety levels. There is a definite advantage to running a group for a block of time, both for continuity and cohesion, and in relationship to the material being dealt with, although dramatherapists who do not usually have co-workers may have to consider that a weekend workshop can be quite exhausting, despite debriefing and process supervision. There continues to be some healthy debate over the best form of treatment available for PTSD: whether behaviour therapy, neurolinguistic programming or creative therapies should be used. I believe that within therapy there is a place for both thought and feeling, and integration and acknowledgement of this can lead to a more holistic approach. Turner (1982) describes two poles of meaning: the 'ideological' and the 'sensory'. The ideological pole represents the norms and values for the maintenance of political, social and domestic life, whereas the sensory arouses the emotions and collective representations of human feelings. When they are brought into contact with one another, one reinforces the other.

All groupwork contains certain dramatic elements – the formal psychotherapy group, for instance, uses the most primitive theatre form, the circle. However, dramatherapy groups can make use of various other techniques not, perhaps, usually addressed in other forms of group work. For example, in PTSD groups I make use of spectograms, role-reversal, active exploration and guided imagery, as well as the metaphors given by the group, and poetry and story-telling in addition to collage work and photography. Using one of these methods as an illustration, the following are examples of group sessions that I have facilitated using spectograms:

Statement
Comments

Communication breakdown
Mother going further away
but he's still aware of her out
of corner of his eye
Wife has turned her back on
his mother
Distance between him and wife
Always been close to brother
and sister, but separated
geographically
In-laws closer than mother.
Father-in-law substitutes for
his father

* = 'distance'

From left to right the figures represent: Alan's brother, his sister, his mother. himself, his wife, his father-in-law, his mother-in-law and his sister-in-law.

Note: The 'distance' between Alan and his wife.

Figure 6.1a: Alan's spectogram – himself in relation to significant others

From left to right the figures represent: Alan's brother, his mother, his sister, himself, his wife, his sister-in-law, his mother-in-law and his father-in-law.

Note: Alan and his wife are touching.

Statement	Confronting the problem
Comments	Would like himself and wife to be touching, side by side
	Family in circle so they can all communicate with one another as they want/need
Outcome	Asked wife to make spectogram to compare perceptions and discuss more understanding of dynamic and need for communication

Figure 6.1b: How Alan wishes to be

Nigel is represented by the bird (an eagle); in front of him are his two adult children and the dog and to the right is his wife.

Statement   Freedom

Comments   Out floating around, taking a good look at things, 'free'

Figure 6.2a: Nigel's spectogram – himself in relation to significant others

Nigel is represented by the bird. *In front of him from left to right are:* One of his grown-up children, his dog, his other grow-up child and his wife.

Statement	Uncertainty
Comments	Himself 'in charge', 'provider'
	Family looking up to him
Development	Challenged by group members about his prime place and conceded that he would have to come down at times for food (added 'nourishment'). Discussed family's contribution. Disclosed on feelings of failure/isolation, used metaphor of crossroads with traffic-lights

Figure 6.2b: Nigel's spectrogram of how he would prefer things to be

From left to right are Keith: 'as he was' (a dinosaur), 'as a pig', 'as an elephant', as 'Keith'. At the far right of the picture is his wife with the family safe inside her.

Statement	Sorry
Comments	The dinosaur is how I was, I've left it behind
	The pig and elephant come back every now and then, but they're getting left behind
	I'm closer to my wife – can travel to and fro between space I can look back and see where I've come from
	My wife is very strong, has kept things together, I recognise that now

Figure 6.3a: Keith's spectogram – himself in relation to significant others

From left to right are: Keith, his wife, and in front of his wife are Keith's parents.

Statement   Watch this space

Comments   Like to be touching wife, mutual support. No significance in size now, protecting and caring for our children. Close to parents again. I'm getting there

Figure 6.3b: Keith's spectogram – how he would prefer things to be

From left to right the figures are: Brian's baby, his child, his wife and then on the far right himself. The wool signifies a barrier.

Statement   Barrier

Comments   A 'barrier' all of his own making, all his fault.

Wife left looking after children

Don't know him

Figure 6.4a: Brian's spectogram – himself in relation to significant others

From left to right the figures are: Brian's baby, his young child, his wife
and himself.

Statement   Confusion/Courage

Comments   Barrier gone. By his wife's side and close to
                   children – but out of the funny clothes! Felt it was
                   very difficult to get rid of barrier, although some
                   improvement already made. With help of group
                   decided that he could already see through parts of
                   barrier and that it would be possible to dismantle
                   it, a bit at a time and that partner could and would
                   help.

Figure 6.4b: Brian's spectogram 'How he would like things to be'

From left to right: the two larger dolls are Peter's father and mother. The smaller dolls at the front are Peter's three older brothers, his wife, his two-year-old daughter and himself.

Statement	Disappointment and distance
Comments	Distance between himself and mother – mother looking other way, more interested in brothers, who had never done as well as him. (Talked of total breakdown in communication between mother and himself since PTSD. Vented considerable anger and jealousy of brothers)

Figure 6.5a: Peter's spectogram himself in relation to significant others

From left to right: the two larger dolls are Peter's father and mother. The smaller dolls at the front are Peter's three older brothers, his wife, his child and himself.

Statement	Disappointment
Comments	Would prefer to be close to mother and brothers. Father more part of it, but Peter's family unit to remain slightly separate
Outcome	Much deliberation – felt mother in wrong so he should make first move. Group suggested alternative approaches and Peter was able to express regret and sense of loss with situation also identified with some of mother's possible feelings. Decided to explain to her how he felt and then see response

Figure 6.5b: Peter's spectogram of how he would prefer things to be

In group work a structure is very important for the reasons discussed earlier. I usually work with the model provided by the 'key concepts of treatment' described in Chapter 5. The following points, however, also need consideration:

1. *How many sessions are to be held?* I would recommend in the region of eight, to allow time to look at related issues arising at the present time, in addition to the material that initially brought the members into the group.

   In final sessions, the termination of the group and the sense of loss this may cause (which may mirror other losses) may also require exploration, acknowledgement and some sort of resolution or acceptance.

2. *How long will each session last?* This depends on the format if the 'warm-up – development – closure' structure is used, then 2–2¹⁄₂ hours seems reasonable to achieve some intensity to the work in the developmental phase. It is essential each time to pay attention to the warm-up phase so that the people can enter the space and identify either physically or in their imagination a 'safe space' within the room. Highly charged emotions may be released, even though they may not be fully expressed, so a third of the time should be spent in closure, group sharing and support, with the facilitator ensuring that people feel safe to leave.

3. *How many people in the group?* This depends on circumstances, but taking the intense nature of such a group into account, four to six is a good number – ideally with some common ground, such as accident victims, battle stress casualties or burn sufferers.

4. *Where should the session take place?* It is important that the venue is large enough for dramatic work to take place, that it is free from interruptions and that it affords privacy for the group. I also find it helpful to have a variety of materials available, such as:

   • Sand boxes – for the recreation of events and images

   • Small figures – animals of every conceivable species; people figures – including babies and young children of different ethnic origins; trees, gates, houses; cars, ambulances, fire-engines, police-cars, tractors and other discarded toy box items.

Miniature objects seem to fascinate and condense power, but also to make, by their very smallness, the person holding them more powerful (Casson 1991). These small items are particularly useful for projective work, as there is both a distancing and a containment when people use them as a way of telling their story. Often, they become conscious of dynamics that they were not previously conscious of as they position their figures and relate to what they are doing. I often ask people to work in pairs and to take it in turns to use the trays: the person observing then can listen to the story and may question things such as distances between figures or objects, directions they face and any significance perceived by the storyteller. The observer should not, however, interpret or assume – her chief role is to listen – but she can help in the de-roling. Groups often find it helpful to have photographs of their sculpts for future reference. Before such a session begins the dramatherapist should explain both this and the importance and necessity of de-roling the figures. A simple way of doing this is to place the objects on a chair and say for example, 'This is no longer my father, this object is a cow', or 'this is no longer the ambulance that took me to hospital, this model is a matchbox toy'.

The dramatherapist's role throughout these sessions includes setting time boundaries, reminding people five minutes before it is time to swap, and ensuring de-roling is carried out. She has to be aware of what takes place in the sub groups, and to clarify and enable as required. At the end of the exercise, the group can come together and share with each other what they wish. This exercise has an additional benefit in that it requires people to listen to others – in PTSD the sufferer often becomes self-absorbed and oblivious to others' needs.

In addition to the sand trays and miniature figures I find it useful to have the following readily available: art materials; large rolls of paper; containers, ranging from intricate small trinket holders to large cardboard boxes; fabric – long pieces covering a wide choice of colours and textures; musical instruments; cushions; various sets of Russian dolls; plasticine; a wide variety of photographs; books and magazines; paper batons; audio tapes and players; video tapes and players; a camera; candles; buttons; collage materials; a wooden cross; a mother of pearl cross; dried flowers.

The following section concludes this chapter by providing an example of a workshop designed for therapists who wanted to find out more about the use of dramatherapy in Post Traumatic Stress Disorder. Experiential learning about groupwork and PTSD is important so that therapists who plan to work in this way are aware of the ways in which subconscious, traumatic material may be accessed, and of the necessity of providing a clear structure to facilitate a sense of safety during the session. This session can also be used in the treatment of PTSD sufferers. The workshop lasted for half a day and the group consisted of eight people.

When we met I first clarified what the participants' expectations were, and whether they had worked as a group before – they had. I then outlined the workshop and gave them a choice of doing personal work or basing it on clients known to them. They all opted for personal work.

Activity	Rationale
Individuals form a circle. One person mimes an activity that they had to do in order to get to the session. The person next to them (clockwise) copies the action and then mimes an activity of their own. The next person then copies the second person's activity and adds their own, and so on until each person has had a turn.	Action begun – leaving the 'outside' world and developing a sense of group.
Clarify/share expectations of workshop.	Confusion is minimised. Structure of session is made known. Feeling of mutability yet safety is engendered.
Each person explores the room and finds a 'safe' space where he feels comfortable and feels he can return to any time he needs during workshop.	Sets boundaries and gives the participants a sense of control. Creates a sense of anticipation of the work to come.

Activity

In the circle an imaginary ball is passed that can change shape, texture or weight at the thrower's command.

The group gets into pairs, and each spend two minutes sharing with their partners why they are here. (*Note*: the facilitator keeps time throughout the session giving reminders before the time limit is reached and when to change roles with the partner.)

Taking it in turns with the partner (25 minutes each), each person uses sand trays and whatever he or she selects from a wide range of objects and figures to create a spectogram.

When the spectogram is complete, the story is shared with the partner. The partner listens and only asks clarifying questions.

The objects are de-roled. The partner ensures that this is done and may assist in it.

The partners swap over a repeat the activities, with the other partner's story.

Rationale

Engages the imaginative process, releases tension and creates laughter.

Allows each to establish what they have in common and what their differences are. Gives the experience of being listened to, and listening.

Sand trays allow for the containment and distancing of the matter being explored. This can lead to a greater number of explanations. The handling, choice and use of objects stimulates the imagination and inhibits cognitive 'censoring'.

The story is listened to, but the partner does not interpret it. It is important to give the person a sense that what he says really matters and is not trivial, and therefore it should not be interpreted through someone else's experiences and perceptions.

Level of work can be deep: this can prevent unwanted lasting associations occurring. It also gives space and time to return to the present.

Activity	Rationale
Using a wide selection of materials: magazines, paints, pens and a large sheet of card, the group make a collage reflecting their experiences and hopes (30 minutes).	The group comes together for mutual support and sharing.
Opportunity to add to collage.	Refocusing and de-roling from the previous activity.
The original partners sit back to back, close their eyes and become aware of anything they either want to explore further or leave behind (5 minutes).	Provides mutual comfort, slows down the pace, and allows for reflection on what has taken place.
The partners slowly turn around to face each other, touching hands, and share what they want to (10 minutes).	Brings the group back to the 'here and now'.
The group forms a large circle. Each person makes a brief statement of what they want to take with them. They also have the opportunity to throw into an imaginary pit in the centre of the circle what they want to leave behind (20 minutes).	Provides mutual support. Allows each person to focus on the experience and gives them the opportunity to recognise needs and the opportunity to discard negative emotions.
Break for refreshments (20 minutes).	Gives everyone the opportunity to be 'themselves', allows for transition to the next part of workshop and gives times to digest what has taken place so far.

Activity	Rationale
Introduction of the theme of moving forward. The group decide whether to explore in a large group or sub-groups (this group decided on large group). They can use mime, dance, or storytelling. There are two rules: respect one another's safety and respect one another's wish to opt out at any stage of the journey. They can only move forward across room – *not* backwards (30 minutes).	This is a key concept in PTSD. It gives responsibility to the group, and necessitates them making choices and implementing communication, negotiating and problem-solving skills.

This particular group of dramatherapists presented a very powerful work involving the use of metaphor, noise, and much mutual assistance. At times I was thankful that the safety rule had been made, as there may otherwise have been risk of physical injury during the catheric period in which they gave vent to previously suppressed emotions. The production reached a very moving resolution during the following closure phase.

Everyone in the circle links hands and makes eye contact with each other. They drop hands and leave the circle as themselves.	Enables the acknowledgement of individuality within the group and the acknowledgement of self.

The workshop illustrated to the dramatherapists the use and importance of structure when working with trauma. Rather than stifling the work done, the structure allowed for greater exploration. The key concepts outlined in Chapter 5 were embodied within the structure.

Conclusion

Group work is of benefit in treating PTSD because it enables participants to share their experiences. Although each individual's perception is different, even if they have all been involved in the same incident, there is usually a common thread linking them together. The problems in adaptation and behaviour that occur after a traumatic incident are often similar in a wide range of people, and the sharing of both the problems and the approaches to coping with and resolving them can be an enormous help in their struggle towards leading a fuller life. Feelings of isolation are particularly acute in PTSD, and once people have got over the initial hurdle involved in sharing and sometimes reliving their experience with others the sense of being alone fades and is replaced with a sense of journeying together. It is often a privilege for the therapist to witness the support that is offered in a group, and the ability of one person to put aside their own difficulties in order to assist someone else through theirs is a sign of the growth that people can achieve while receiving group treatment.

In addition to facilitating this support, groupwork also enables certain unhelpful behaviours to be challenged. For example, if someone resorts to drinking heavily and uses PTSD as the reason, others also diagnosed as suffering from PTSD can say with experience whether this is reasonable or whether it is actually destructive behaviour that is an attempt to mask the pain of the individual.

The use of dramatherapy in groups has the benefit of being able to work at different levels from purely verbal therapy, in which people can get bogged down by semantics – they are able to talk about what happened on an intellectual plane, but it is completely devoid of meaning or emotion. (Several of my clients, whose plight has been the subject of media speculation and who themselves have been the subject of many media interviews, have said how they had got used to simply chanting their story and were, as a result, totally divorced from what it actually meant within.) The participants in a dramatherapy group eventually have to leave the group and re-establish themselves within their social setting, and their experience of the group means that they have already had the opportunity to be creative, try out new ideas and test whether the recounting of their experiences can be borne by others who will be supportive and not judgmental of them: they have had the chance to explore their new 'world picture' and the various responses they can make to it.

CHAPTER 7

The Use of Dramatherapy in the Treatment of Individuals Suffering from PTSD

Give sorrow words: the grief that does not speak
Whispers the o'erfraught heart, and bids it break.

Macbeth, IV.3.

Although dramatherapy makes use of the group, much of the creative process involved can be used in a relationship between the therapist and an individual client. If we recognise that in each of us there are a number of sub-personalities or different facets, then our inner world can be thought of as a stage on which various conflicts, arguments and dialogues are carried out – there is interaction and there are inter-relationships. The dramatherapy process provides an opportunity for the individual to experiment with various possibilities, to re-experience and clarify perceptions of past events, aided by the dramatherapist, who supplies the structure or the container for what takes place.

In the treatment of PTSD the presence of others with similar experiences in a group usually has a positive effect on the outcome and reduces the sense of isolation, but given that this is not always possible due to resources or the client's reluctance to disclose information to others, individual treatment using dramatherapy can also have a successful outcome.

Initial assessment interview

The purpose of this interview is to discover with individuals what they feel their main difficulties are and to decide whether they fit the diagnostic criteria for PTSD.

This interview includes the completion of the General Health Questionnaire (General Practice Research Unit 1978), the HSW Scale of Reactions to an Accident or Disaster, and the Indices of Coping Responses questionnaire (see Figures 7.1 and 7.2).

Figure 7.1: HSW Scale
Reactions to an Accident or a Disaster

Below you will find twelve statements commonly found among people who have been involved in an accident or a disaster. Please indicate two things to each statement: (1) how you have felt AT WORST and (2) how you feel TODAY. Indicate your answers by encircling either YES or NO, whatever seems right about yourself. Please give your two answers to all the statements.

	At Worst		*Today*	
1. Difficulties with sleep	YES	NO	YES	NO
2. Nightmares about the event	YES	NO	YES	NO
3. Depressed mood	YES	NO	YES	NO
4. Tendencies to jump or startle at sudden noises or moves	YES	NO	YES	NO
5. Irritable feelings (I am easily getting irritable or angry)	YES	NO	YES	NO
6. Unstable mood; frequent ups and downs	YES	NO	YES	NO
7. Bad conscience, self-accusations or guilt	YES	NO	YES	NO
8. Fears of situations that may initiate memories of the event	YES	NO	YES	NO
9. Tensions in my body	YES	NO	YES	NO
10. Impaired memory	YES	NO	YES	NO
11. Difficulties in concentrating	YES	NO	YES	NO

Figure 7.2: Indices of Coping Responses

Please indicate which of the following you did in connection with this event:

	No	YES Once or Twice	YES Some-times	YES Fairly Often
1. Tried to find out more about the situation	☐	☐	☐	☐
2. Talked with spouse or other relative about the problem	☐	☐	☐	☐
3. Talked with friend about the problem	☐	☐	☐	☐
4. Talked with professional person (e.g. doctor, lawyer, clergy)	☐	☐	☐	☐
5. Prayed for guidance and/or strength	☐	☐	☐	☐
6. Prepared for the worst	☐	☐	☐	☐
7. Didn't worry about it, figured everything would probably work out	☐	☐	☐	☐
8. Took it out on other people when I felt angry or depressed	☐	☐	☐	☐
9. Tried to see the positive side of the situation	☐	☐	☐	☐
10. Got busy with other things to keep my mind of the problem	☐	☐	☐	☐
11. Made a plan of action and followed it	☐	☐	☐	☐
12. Considered several alternatives for handling the problem	☐	☐	☐	☐

Figure 7.2: Indices of Coping Responses (continued)

	No	YES Once or Twice	YES Some- times	YES Fairly Often
13. Drew on my past experiences; I was in a similar situation before	☐	☐	☐	☐
14. Kept my feelings to myself	☐	☐	☐	☐
15. Took things a day at a time, one step at a time	☐	☐	☐	☐

In addition to this I compare the client's signs and symptoms with the DSM criteria (see Chapter 1). Some workers have asked whether presenting these scales causes further distress, but on the contrary I have found that people are often relieved to find what they have been experiencing occurs amongst other individuals. These scales help to provide a baseline from which to work. I stress that they should be used as an aid to understanding the person's difficulties and not as a 'screen' that distances the therapist from the other person in the space.

The interview needs to elicit the following information:

- The client's expectations and perceived needs
- The dramatherapist's response
- Level of depression
- Any suicidal ideation
- Current level of functioning
- Coping mechanisms
- Any support network
- Somatic problems
- Length of time since incident
- Any previous traumas

- Sleep disturbance
- Help being received.

The client's expectations and perceived needs

This helps to ascertain whether the client has sought help of his or her own volition or has been coerced by a concerned family. Often a crisis situation has triggered them to seek help, for example, a spouse who can no longer tolerate the person's behaviour and who has threatened to leave. It may emerge that the client really just wants the therapist to give him an excuse to continue as he is: this may involve drinking alcohol excessively, isolating himself or being physically violent. Alternatively they may want the dramatherapist to wave a magic-wand and make things as they were before (this is a very negative view and most people can progress from this). Others come because they are ready to take their first step in moving forward.

The dramatherapist's response

Just as each client is unique, so is each therapist in his or her approaches and responses. However, the trained dramatherapist has a code of ethics (BADth 1991) as well as often being governed by other professional codes such as the UKCC Code of Conduct for Registered Nurses (UKCC 1992). It is assumed that she would not enter into this type of work unless adequately prepared – having the right equipment for the journey, being competent in using it and being aware of when another 'route' or type of treatment or therapist is needed. In keeping with what I have expressed elsewhere in the book, I aim for clarity in this assessment interview.

I will acknowledge that I recognise that the person's distress may be reflected in his or her behaviour during sessions, but that I will expect him to control any possible violence to others, themselves, or property. If the person is given the message that the therapist believes he is capable of controlling his own behaviour, this will contribute to a sense of self-empowerment. An agreement to refrain from violence is a basic ground rule that forms part of the foundations on which the framework of treatment (see Chapter 5) can rest securely. (It may also be noted that if, for example, clients are from a military back-ground they and others may be at risk of physical harm if there is not this 'holding', nurturing environment, due to their expertise in physical combat). When people express the wish that I could make things as they were before the traumatic event, if I also feel that wish, for example when a child has been killed, then I will say so (it seems best to be honest and accepting of their desperation). Gently I say that it is not possible and that I have no magic powers, but ensure that I am prepared to be there, with them, if they want.

Level of depression/anxiety

A dramatherapist should have a knowledge of what constitutes clinical depression or severe anxiety. If the depression is severe it may affect the client's ability to work in the session.

PTSD commonly causes a reactive depression. If the therapist is in doubt as to whether separate treatment for this is required then, with the client's permission, she should discuss it with the person providing medical care or encourage the client to do so. Someone who is acutely anxious often responds well once started on a treatment programme. The anxiety may well be tied to what happened when the traumatic incident took place and symptoms may therefore be different. For example, someone who was caught in a bomb explosion may have an exaggerated startle response.

Suicidal ideation

A common symptom of PTSD is the feeling that the person should have died at the time of the incident. Some sufferers feel they are already dead and so nothing they do to themselves can be worse, and some feel they were responsible for injuries sustained by others. As a result they begin a downward spiral where suicide becomes, to them, a real option. A competent dramatherapist should be able to assess risk factors and decide upon an appropriate course of action, or to seek a second opinion. If the person is being treated on an out-patient basis I ask her to involve her personal support network. She can usually identify someone willing to be with her. I contract with them to make contact with this person, myself or a GP before acting on impulse. Some clients have commented that this has made them feel safer and given them a feeling of an external influence to keep check on their impulses.

If a dramatherapist is concerned about the level of risk a client is at, she must liaise with the GP or psychiatrist. I have never found that a distressed client has objected when I have said I thought it necessary that he or she should receive further help. If people are in a high-risk state, however, this does not preclude them from using dramatherapy as a form of treatment for PTSD, and it may be an indication that they wish to change.

It is imperative that there is clarity of approach in the work, with the session well-structured and attention paid to the closure to ensure that the client feels 'safe' to leave. It is also important to ensure, by discussing with clients or other members of staff involved with them, that their support network is still intact and coping. If the client is an in-patient, it is important to let the other staff know how the session has gone.

Current level of functioning

What is the person doing in terms of daily living activities? Has this changed? Is it improving or getting worse? Is there any psychological impairment, such as concentration, memory, spatial difficulty and so on? How does the client and his or her significant others feel about this?

Coping mechanisms

Has the person experienced anything like this in the past? How did she cope then? How does she manage now? Some people may be using maladaptive coping processes by relying on alcohol, drugs, or withdrawal. However, some defence mechanisms may be valuable, the skilled therapist will utilise and assist the client to build on these to realise their potential. If there are strong defence mechanisms in play it should be remembered that they may actually assist in keeping the person's psyche intact. They, therefore, need to be treated with respect until the client is strong enough to let go of them, otherwise it could be like kicking an unsteady person's crutches away, causing her to crash to the ground.

Support network

Dramatherapy may release intense emotions which should be 'held' in the 'safe container' of the session. However, it will put the client in touch with aspects of himself and his situation that he may have not acknowledged, and the 'process' will continue between sessions. Indeed 'homework' may include finding photographs and press-cuttings, making a collage, writing an account, recording a dream or watching a particular programme that is related to the traumatic event. The support network outside the group may therefore be invaluable in helping the person to share his or her experience. If the client is willing it is often helpful to include significant others within aspects of the treatment. They themselves often have been secondarily affected by the PTSD and may feel helpless. Communication has often suffered and they feel they would like to assist if only they knew how. By not being included they may feel even more distanced from the person in therapy and, therefore, redundant. I make sure I tell people that the first stages of the 'journey' may be difficult, and that treatment can be painful as the individual faces their fear. Several spouses have remarked to me that they felt this was strange thing to say during the initial interview, but three weeks into the treatment, when the client has had a return of nightmares or been crying, they have recalled this comment and not been so alarmed.

If the support network is poor or non-existent the dramatherapist needs to be aware of this. It may be that the client would be better treated in a residential group programme. If clients are ex-services, SSAFA, Naval Family Service or similar organisations may be able to offer support. Alternatively, they may find help from one of the statutory agencies, such as social services, or from clergy, missions or similar, depending on the person's culture and what they will accept.

Somatic problems

Many of the people seen following trauma have physical injuries, some of which may be disfiguring, some of which may affect mobility, and some of which may cause chronic pain and fatigue. Sometimes there are residual affects of head injury which may cause memory impairment, epilepsy, headache and irritability.

The dramatherapist can usefully work in close liaison with physiotherapists to provide holistic treatment for such problems. My tendency is to refer people for full assessment with a view to treatment of physical injury, for optimal functioning and pain relief. Clients comment that as they feel better mentally they feel more able to stay on top of the pain. The body and mind are inextricably linked and it makes sense to treat them both when necessary. Dramatherapy can involve movement work at times and this can be liberating for the participants (the therapist should already be aware from assessment as to the limitations of body work with those with disabilities).

Many people I have worked with have found image relaxation helpful in reducing pain levels. Unlike many muscle-relaxing exercises, the focus is away from the body: the particpant is encouraged to visualise a pleasant scene and then to engage all her senses in enjoying this. An active relaxation that involves shaking out tension from various parts of the body and starts gently but can become vigorous has also often proved helpful. It loosens tense, cramped muscles and joints as well as often causing 'releasing laughter'.

Length of time since incident

There seems to be no upper time limit governing when people do or do not suffer from PTSD: in recent years it has been diagnosed in veterans of the Burma War. There are now two divisions of PTSD:

Acute: onset is less than six months and greater than one month after the incident.

Chronic: symptoms occur more than six months after incident.

The longer the time between the incident and seeking treatment the lengthier the treatment may be. This is in part due to the sufferer having to unlearn unhelpful coping responses that may have become integrated into their lifestyle, such as agoraphobia, alcoholism, or an eating disorder. If this is the case, the dramatherapist may work with a behaviour therapist (if they do not have the necessary skills themselves), who can help the client 'unlearn' these responses. Desensitisation may be a valuable part of the treatment carried out through either behavioural or dramatherapeutic methods, such as role-playing the anxiety provoking situation, and using deep breathing and relaxation to lower the physiological arousal.

Any previous traumas

The PTSD may not altogether be caused by the presented incident. There is often a previous unresolved trauma that has been repressed or blotted out. The client may not be aware of this fact and it may emerge during the assessment ('Is there any time you've experienced similar feelings?') or it may be revealed during the treatment process. The person needs to be reassured that it is all right to bring up this matter, even if it occurred many years previously, otherwise there is a danger they will yet again censor it and so impede recovery.

Sleep disturbance

Sleep disturbance, especially early morning waking, is an indicator of depression. Particularly common in sleep disturbance in cases of PTSD is the presence of intrusive imagery: when the sufferer relaxes to a sufficient extent, imagery relating to sights they have seen during the traumatic incident intrudes. This can rapidly lead to a poor pattern of sleep in which the person tries to avoid reaching this state of relaxation so that the intrusive imagery does not occur.

The use of hypnotic drugs, such as those commonly used from the Benzodiazepine family, can sometimes induce a state in which people are more vulnerable to such imagery. However, anti-depressants, particularly those in the tricyclic group, do seem to help to reduce troublesome imagery. People should be told that such images are a common feature of PTSD, as they often fear that they are actually losing their mind. They should be informed that during treatment these images may at times become more prominent, but that treatment will ultimately help to reduce their frequency and graphic detail.

Help being received

This is to ascertain whether any help has been received from elsewhere, either immediately after the event or at the current time. If other treatment is still running it is important that close liaison is made between all the parties involved to ensure the optimum use of the skills available to the benefit of the client. Such liaison can also be useful in ascertaining whether the client has been unable to sustain treatment or found particular approaches unhelpful, and can lead to a useful discussion about what the client really wants and what his fears about treatment are.

These factors provide a basis from which to work, although I know that some dramatherapists believe in getting into the action straight away, rather than going through this initial process. However, the process is useful for a number of reasons, if, for example, as in many cases, the PTSD sufferer is involved in insurance claims which require records of assessment, treatment and progress for part of the evidence for the claim. The assessment will often take two sessions as it is quite usual for a client to say he does not know how to begin, but then to need to talk non-stop about the trauma – when he has begun telling his story, it is important to listen. Much information for the assessment can be gleaned this way. The therapist should beware of intervening to gain control of the session, as it may be interpreted by the client as 'the therapist was so upset by what I was saying we couldn't go on with it'. This may or may not be a misinterpretation!

The assessment interview can set the flavour for forthcoming work. It is the beginning of a two-way process in which the dramtherapist gives the client the opportunity to express his wants, needs, fears and hopes for the journey and his agreement on how to proceed.

This discussion of the initial assessment shows that much of the work concentrates on information giving. Although it may seem that this does not have much to do with drama, it is vital to have this baseline from which to work, both so that there can be a clarity of approach, and so that good records are kept. It is, however, possible during this assessment to introduce the idea of creative methods of working. A useful way in which to do this is to request that clients make two collages to illustrate how they see themselves in actuality and how they would like to be. As treatment progresses it is always useful to be able to refer back to this stage to remind clients how much they have moved on.

Setting off

The purpose of using dramatherapy in the treatment of PTSD is not to bombard the individual with overwhelming intensity, but to provide him with additional ways to communicate his story. This may be through images, symbols, movement or enactment, in addition to words. Thus, although the person may have a heavy load to carry as he sets out, he is given a greater opportunity to explore, re-arrange and discard that which he no longer needs as he moves forward. Initially a client may not move far from his chair in the therapy room, although he may have travelled a long way in the one-and-a-half-hour session. When musing on this paradox my supervisor reminded me of Peter Brook's quotation: 'I can take an empty space and call it a bare stage. A man walks across this empty space whilst someone else is watching him, and this is all that is needed for an act of theatre to be engaged' (Brook 1972).

In early sessions I make much use of projective work, in particular sand trays (Kalff 1980) and spectograms.

The sand tray measures 57cm x 72cm x 7cm. This is thought to be an appropriate size, as it can be viewed at once by the sculptor. It is also a 'safe container' in which to tell the story and allows distancing between the sculptor and the portrayal. It is good to keep a diagram or photograph of the early sculpt so that the client can compare it with later ones (this is often requested by the client towards the termination of the therapy). The dramatherapist can use sand-pictures to determine progress, recurring images or mental blocks. In the case of a 'block', it is a good starting point.

> Therapist: I notice Tom [*client*] is still standing with a shut gate between him and the family.
>
> Tom: Yes, the gate's still there. The padlock has gone though.
>
> Therapist: Does the gate open ever?
>
> Tom: It's been shut so long it only opens with a push.
>
> Therapist: How would Tom like the gate to be?
>
> Tom: [*moves the gate open and takes the figure Tom through it. Long pause...*] So he can move back and forth when he wants.
>
> Therapist: The gate can be opened after all if Tom pushes it.

Tom: Mmm...

The figures were de-roled by Tom.

Tom was witness to a fatal road accident. He fulfilled the diagnostic criteria for PTSD and had sought help when his increasing withdrawal from the family had caused his wife to threaten to leave him. She and his children were supportive of his treatment. In several later sessions Tom reconstructed the sand picture and explored ways of 'opening the gate' and 'oiling the hinges' with his family assisting and coming through to his area; 'propping the gate open' and so on. In one piece of work he, through role-play, became a gate, and was able to give voice to how the gate felt, and what its purpose was. What originally seemed a 'block' through Tom's own creativity became a 'stepping-stone' in a powerful, transformative way.

Any reader not familiar with dramatherapy may see this account as full of possibilities for analysis, or interpretation of the client. However, when working with metaphor in this way the client needs to 'process' it for himself, and analyse what perspective it gives him, not the therapist.

It needs to be made clear in the initial contract that the aim of the session is to explore something together rather than explain things. When a client creates a sculpt or other life picture, they enter an exploratory dramatic structure, re-creating a scene in the drama of their life like a miniature theatre (Jennings 1990).

A sand-picture can also be useful in identifying the support network. A young woman was referred for dramatherapy ostensibly for an 'eating disorder'. Assessment revealed that she had developed her food avoidance and ritualistic behaviour after being raped by a stranger at a party six months previously.

She had not contacted the police as she had been drunk at the time and she felt that must have deserved the rape. She had recently contacted a rape helpline and was considering seeking further support from them. She had said that she didn't know if she could carry on much longer and they had encouraged her to seek immediate help.

She said she had not considered suicide but just knew something had to happen. She had divorced herself from her physical body; hence her restrictions on eating (she had no previous history of difficulties with food) may be seen as:

- over-distancing and denial of bodily feelings
- a somatic effect of grief
- an attempt to have control over something in her life.

She had also become ritualistic, repeatedly-washing herself and never feeling the task complete. She vividly described how she had vomited following the rape and had taken five successive baths and burnt the clothes she had been wearing. Although her friends were concerned about her, she was avoiding them, lest they too become contaminated.

This woman was clearly in a state of acute distress, and yet able to give a clear account. She acknowledged her need and willingness for help. Of immediate concern to me as the dramatherapist was the identification of a supportive network so that she would begin to feel secure in the present time. After a brief explanation I asked her to use the sand tray and choose from a wide range of figures and objects to portray herself in relation to significant others. She worked intently and used over thirty figures for her network. She chose a rhino as herself and other animal figures for most other people, with clown figures for some of those who made her happy. She remarked that she was surprised how many people were important to her, since if I had asked her outright she thought she may have said 'no one'. She explained the importance of various groupings to me. She was able to explore who was close to her at the moment, and from that, whom she felt she could talk to about what she was experiencing, and what had happened to her. This was a college friend whom she had known for ten years and had shared growing-up with. The figures were finally de-roled and she was given an appointment to see me again four days later, so that we could work out together a treatment programme. She had also decided to contact the rape helpline with view to meeting someone who had had a similar experience.

When she came to see me, in view of the suspected 'high-risk' in terms of self-harm, it was important to have a structured approach and to assist her with immediate problem-solving. The use of the sand-picture in identifying the network meant that the picture was soon clear to me, whereas it may have taken several sessions if done in a verbal way. It also seemed that it bypassed the woman's switched-off cognitions and negativity, freeing her to identify those who could support her.

A more directive approach, similar to the model often used in crisis intervention work, may also be used. In this case, the focus is purely on the 'here and now' and on structuring the person's day one step at a time. In *Crisis Intervention Verbatim* Nira Kfir (1982) describes this model of intervention more fully, but its essential elements are:

1. *Giving concrete information.* Those experiencing a crisis do not want to ponder on the mysteries of life or the development of personality; they are often unable to grasp the abstract or take an overall view of their situation. They require assistance in getting through the next hour, and need clear, concise information aimed at reducing anxiety. Such information may include details of: sources of help available; similar situations; norms and standards expected in such situations; the therapist's assessment of what the client is experiencing; what can be done; how long the feelings will last; chances of recurrence; and future prognosis as the crisis subsides. It is always helpful to provide written information (or recorded if the person has difficulties with reading), as they may find they cannot recall what has been said.

2. *Providing support by involvement.* Any involvement can provide support – simply by being with a person who is experiencing difficulties can tell her that she is all right. Practical actions, such as providing respite from their normal obligations and providing guidance are all of value, and it should be remembered that no one person has a monopoly on giving this sort of support.

3. *Providing alternatives and immediate concrete activities.* Sometimes the solution that a person wants may not be possible, for example a parent who wishes his dead child to be alive again. In such cases, rather than being swamped by a sense of helplessness, the therapist should help the person to find activities to help him get through their crisis one step at a time. Structuring daily activities, even at the level of resting, washing and so on, can be useful here, as it can help the person focus on the activity in hand, rather than on the events that have caused his crisis.

This method may be used with well-structured dramatherapy as one facet of the treatment. This, and the additional involvement of other agencies such as rape crisis centres, can help to provide a more holistic approach, giving the client increased options for help and support as well as the opportunity to meet with others who have experienced and survived similar situations.

Case study – AB

(One-hour-long sessions)

AB is a 47-year-old policeman. He answered a routine call to attend at the scene of a sudden death. When he arrived he found a man hanging, and it was apparent he had intended to take his own life. He knew the man and his family, but only vaguely. For three months following this AB was troubled by flashbacks and sleepless nights. His wife was concerned about his preoccupation and persuaded him to make contact with me. When screened it was apparent that AB was suffering from PTSD.

Session 1

During the initial session AB recounted his story of events, from the day he went on duty, to his attendance at the Coroner's Court. He went into graphic detail about the body, describing sight, sound, smell and fear, together with some expression of anger at 'having to clear up someone else's mess'. He did not have a close colleague to share these feelings with and refrained from telling his wife about the events as she was pregnant with their first child and he didn't want to distress her. He expressed a sense of relief at being able to tell his story.

AB was experiencing panic attacks and I explained basic anxiety management skills and the 'fight or flight' response (see Key Concepts, Chapter 5). He practised a short relaxation technique (discussed later in this chapter), in which he concentrated on his breathing: he imagined breathing in cleansing breath and breathing out the tensions he wanted to get rid of. The imagery was guided (Figley and Sprenkle 1978) and non-threatening (in PTSD intrusive images can be a source of distress and this must be borne in mind when using relaxation in early stages of treatment). AB was given an audio tape of the relaxation imagery to help him practise this skill between sessions.

Session 2

I explained to AB that it would be helpful to get a picture of how things were in relation to him and others in his life. He chose two sets of Russian dolls to illustrate this. He laid one doll close to him on its side, and once he had placed the others he described his spectogram, explaining who was represented and why they were placed where they were.

When he came to the figure lying on its side, he described him as a paternal uncle whom he had felt close to and who had shot himself at the age of 26, when AB was 10. His family had hardly spoken of him since the incident and had never answered any questions. He had asked to go to the funeral but had been told he was too young, and he had instead been sent to a relative in another country for a two-week holiday. When he came back he remembers the photographs of his uncle had been taken off his grandmother's sideboard. AB said that when he had attended the recent suicide it had came into his mind how lonely and desperate it was to die in this way. He had been taken by surprise at the extent of his grief, apparently towards a near-stranger, and his recall of a tragedy that had taken place 17 years ago. AB became tearful when talking about his uncle, and commented that he would not usually let himself cry about it. He had not been aware of any of his family crying at the time of his uncle's death. He said he felt it may be helpful to look at these things in more depth.

Session 3

(Two hours long by prior agreement)

The third session was started by AB saying he and his parents had been able to talk about his father's feelings of sorrow. He said that he felt he wanted to remember the happier things about his uncle. I had asked AB to try and find any photographs or keepsakes to do with his uncle. He was able to obtain some of these from his mother, including a photo of his uncle as a baby, and a pocket-knife.

After looking at all the photographs and encouraging AB to comment on each, I asked him to pick one and describe it in depth, and how it made him feel. AB picked one of his uncle aged about 18 in which he had a push-bike and was laughing at the photographer (AB's father). He began first describing the photograph and then started talking to his uncle, saying 'you seem happy' and 'you must have known me by then; I was two'.

We then moved into 'empty chair' work, where AB addressed his uncle as if he were in the chair. He became quite involved in this one-way conversation and asked questions such as 'Why?' before making the statement 'I love you still and miss you – I wish you were here to see the new baby'. He became tearful but finished his conversation by saying goodbye. He said he had been unaware of the sense of loss he felt over his uncle. He was pleased to have in his possession some of the keepsakes relating to his past. He said it was his intention to share some of the memories with his wife, who had been feeling shut out from his emotions (Keubler-Ross 1970). The session closed with AB focusing on what had taken place by shutting his eyes and visualising his uncle walking away from him down a street and turning back to wave before going round a corner. He then spent a few minutes in relaxation. We had discussed the problem of unre-solved grief and the fact that someone can become emotionally 'stuck' until something triggers a memory.

Session 4

This session concentrated on how AB would deal with a similar situation arising in his duties. He identified positive aspects of his own experience and how it may have enabled him to support col-leagues and relatives. A role-play was set up using a couple of assistants to take on the roles of a parent and a police colleague who had to break the news after finding a body. AB set the scene, thereby giving him a feeling of some control over events. He elected to describe graphically a suicide by hanging (the dramatherapy assis-tants were prepared for this possibility beforehand). He then took on the role of breaking the news and answering the parent's questions. Afterwards he proceeded to counsel and assist his colleague in debriefing. During the scene with the relatives he felt some anxiety symptoms, but practised deep breathing and was pleased that he maintained control. The scene lasted thirty minutes, after which all the participants were de-roled. In keeping with debriefing, the assis-tants met with me afterwards to ensure they were de-roled and to ensure that they had the opportunity to express their feelings and thoughts about what had just taken place. AB and I met for two further sessions, to consolidate the experiences of this previous session, and for guidance as necessary through the grieving process.

As I have reflected on some of the journeys that I have travelled with clients, various remarks have come back to me which I think serve as illustrations of both the dilemmas and the joys of transformation:

'What if I remember and then can't forget?'

'I thought I'd never get through that day – it all came back to me. I got through though, now I know there are times I can feel better.'

'I don't want to forget the person who died. If I acknowledge him, I feel he will give me more space.'

'In that sculpt I realised that as I was facing my attacker all the time (though saying I wasn't), I was turning my back on my wife.'

'I don't want to forget my child, and you don't tell me to put her behind me. This paying tribute, I understand it now – that's what I want to do.'

'The void, emptiness I felt inside is where the old me died. Now I feel something new is growing there and I'm glad.'

'After the accident I thought Jesus was for children, but now I know he's been with me all the time and I can even pray sometimes.'

'I feel like I did when I was adolescent – testing the ground, having new conflicts and having to find new solutions to them.'

These journeys are arduous and can take unexpected turns, and the life journey carries on far beyond the span of treatment for PTSD. It is hoped, however, that this makes the travellers more aware of their resources to help themselves and others onward.

Creativity is often a by-product of the treatment and it is not unusual for those who have initially expressed reluctance or reserve to take up some hobby such as writing, poetry, painting, drama, dance, as they have discovered a freedom to express themselves and a growth in confidence.

Relaxation and dramatherapy

Whether working with a group or an individual, from early on in this treatment it is important to help the clients to relax. Before selecting the most useful type of relaxation for each individual the therapist must be aware of any triggers that may prevent the person being able to relax, and also observe any difficulties that may occur during sessions. For example, someone who has been raped may find the standard relaxation position of lying down most distressing. A soldier whose trauma has been provoked by having to lie in confined spaces during active service may also be distressed. Some people say that whenever they have been asked to clear their minds and relax they have found intrusive imagery becomes very prominent and disturbing. Some people have physical injuries that, although they may be healed, still restrict mobility or cause pain. The majority of people I have worked with report that they have found guided imagery to be most relaxing. I find out from them about any particular images that they find enjoyable or relaxing, as well as any particular scenes or situations that they would find frightening or difficult, for example some people love images of the sea, while for others it is perhaps associated with the incident that has led them to come for treatment. In a relaxation session the group are given a choice of whether to lie down supported by pillows, blankets or bean bags, or to sit in comfortable chairs.

One of the methods that I use to help release tension and induce a relaxed feeling is through movement. I often use this to begin a group session, but it can also be used with individuals and many clients report that they find it beneficial when they are alone as well. This includes some people who have physical difficulties but adapt the exercises to suit them. They report that it often reduces the tense feelings in their muscles and consequently reduces the pain they feel. I always emphasise to them that it is important that they start fairly slowly to warm up the muscles and not to put strain on to any part of their body. A typical session is as follows:

Tension releaser

In a circle, stretch up through your body without raising your shoulders. Be aware of any tension as you stretch up. Imagine your body feeling lighter and then just let go.

Pick out parts of your body, beginning with your hands, and just slowly shake them, shaking out some of the tension, let that shaking movement spread through your body. Keeping all movements loose, kick out your legs and imagine who or what you are kicking, continue to let your body shake and flop, checking for any tension (for example in your jaw, back of neck, shoulders or knee joints): shrug off these areas of tension.

Gently roll your shoulders and roll your head gently from side to side. Slow down the movement in your body until it comes to a stop.

Become aware of your breathing. For four cycles of breath, breathe in refreshing, renewing air, breathe out the tension and worries.

Scan your body for any areas that feel tight and give them a final shrug to loosen them up. Be aware of how light and good and renewed you feel. Just enjoy that feeling.

This relaxation should take about ten minutes.

Relaxation imagery

Tapes with the following types of relaxation have proved useful in decreasing arousal and physical pain levels.

Find yourself a comfortable space in which you will not be disturbed. When you are feeling comfortable, please close your eyes. Concentrate on breathing in and breathing out. Do this slowly, be aware of how your body feels against the surface it touches, be aware of any sensations of pressure or heaviness. Scan your body for any areas of tension or tight-ness. Slowly shrug off these areas of tension, peel them away, any areas that feel particularly tense or tight. As you peel them off, in your mind's eye put them in a pile beside you. As you shrug them off be aware of the feeling of lightness. Go back to your breathing in and breathing out. As you breathe in, breathe in refreshing air – as you breathe out, breathe out those tensions you want to let go – do this for five cycles of breath. Each time you breathe out those tensions feel yourself getting lighter and feeling renewed. In your mind's eye focus on a room – this is your own special, safe, secure room; you can decide what is in it. Spend a few moments focusing on the colours in the room, think of the textures, think of any particular fragrances. Are there any particular objects in the room? Any treasures? In this room you feel so peaceful. So secure. Perhaps there are particular things in the room that help you. Spend some time in letting go of any worries or burdens and letting the peace come over you. You can either stay in this room just enjoying the feeling of relaxation, or you can continue on other journeys knowing that this room is yours to return to whenever you want. The time has come perhaps for you to leave your room now: you feel relaxed, the tensions have lifted off you and floated away. In your mind's eye you can take a glance around the room before you prepare to leave. On the count of three you find yourself once more outside the room, aware of the space you are in at this moment, but you carry with you a feeling of serenity. One, two, three. Now give a big stretch out and a big yawn, open your eyes and become aware of where you are now.

Relaxation exercise 2

I want you just to be aware of how you are feeling in your body right now. Close your eyes and be aware of any feelings of heaviness, any feelings of tension or burden. In your mind's eye I want you gradually to take off these tensions or burdens one by one and place them into a rucksack which is beside you. As you peel them off, you feel lighter, but your rucksack becomes heavier and more full, now in your mind's eye the time has come to put your rucksack on and set off on a journey. As you take the rucksack you again become aware of the tension across your shoulders and the heaviness, but you are determined to make this journey and so you plod on, looking at the scenery around you. You are aware of the colours, how your feet feel on the ground, how your body feels, and how the rucksack of your burdens feels. You are aware of the temperature, you are aware of certain smells which bring back different memories.

You walk. As you follow the path you walk through a forest area. Notice how the branches cast shadow, notice the feeling of dampness and the difficulty the sun has in shining through. Pick your way carefully through the area, climbing over a few boulders. Notice how it feels as you touch against them, notice what they mean. Now the path becomes easier and it gradually becomes lighter as the forest gives way to the meadow. You are aware of the sensation of sunshine on your face and the light. You are also aware that the rucksack has become even heavier and so you sit down to rest. You feel the warm ground beneath you – enjoy this peace and the scenery. In your mind's eye you start to explore some of the contents of your rucksack; perhaps some are not so necessary for your journey. Perhaps some things you don't have to carry with you all the time. You go through a sifting process: things that you no longer need you can take out, and in the bottom of your rucksack you find a bright silver shovel. It is really attractive but you didn't know it was there. Now you know you can use it, and you begin to dig a little pit – at first the digging is hard work, but it becomes easier and you feel the goodness of the soil. You take out the things you no longer need and place them one by one in the pit. When you have done this you carefully cover it over again. You put the top soil back, you see something you hadn't noticed that has grow up from the fertilizer you have supplied – it is a beautiful flower. In your mind's eye see what colour that flower is – see the shape, feel the texture of the petals, look at the leaves and be aware of any fragrance. When you have admired the flower, you then think about any discoveries you made whilst going through your rucksack. Perhaps there was a particular thing you discovered and that you would want to look at further, or a treasure you have found. Perhaps it is a feeling rather than an object. Whatever it is, in your mind's eye you produce some very special, delicate paper. Although it is delicate, it is extremely strong and you can parcel up what you want to take with you. Look at the colour of the paper, be aware of the object as you carefully wrap it. You also have with you some fastenings to secure it and you carefully apply them and now you take it in to your hand and you are aware of the positive feelings contained in it. This is for you and you can unwrap it and look at it whenever you want to – it's your secret that gives you strength and courage, you take hold of it carefully and as you get up from where you have been sitting you're aware of that feeling of lightness. Take a look again at the flower before you start on your walk once more.

This time there is a spring in your step and as you breathe in you are aware of the joy of breathing in and just letting go and the pleasure of just being where you are. Now the time has come to return to where you set off – this time you go by a different route. The scenery is really enjoyable – perhaps you meet some people or objects along the way that mean something special to you and you acknowledge them, greet them as you make your way back to the start. This time you are aware that your burden has lifted. It is time to return to your special room taking your treasure with you, and as you enter you are again aware of the familiar surroundings and feelings of peace in your room.

You examine once more the colours and textures of a particular object. You feel safe in the knowledge that you can return to your room whenever you wish or need to, and it is always there for you to just be. You settle yourself down comfortably and soak in the energy and sense of peace...

You enjoy the floating sensation and feeling of lightness, but now the time has come to return to the here and now. So in your mind's eye you glance around the room, you know you can return again and that the room will not change unless you want it to. Now concentrate on your breathing in and breathing out, after three cycles of in-breath and out-breath I want you to give a big stretch and yawn, to leave your room and come back to the space you are in, acknowledging it as a reality, as the now, but you still take with you that feeling of peace.

Further reading

Landy, R. (1986) *Dramatherapy: Concepts and Practice*. Springfield: Charles C. Thomas.

Leick, N. and Davidsen-Nielsen, M. (1991) *Healing Pain: Attachment, Loss and Grief Therapy*. London: Routledge.

CHAPTER 8

Supervision and its Importance

'It's okay going on the journey, but make sure you can always see the light – even if it's only a faint glimmer – so you know the direction to head in.' This was said to me by a supervisor when I was working with someone tragically bereaved and bereft. It was an intuitive remark at a crucial time and one that has stayed with me.

Staying with the journey metaphor, the therapist may also ask herself:

'Have I got the necessary equipment prepared?'

'How about my own luggage – am I able to help carry someone else's in addition to my own?

'If the journey takes different routes, can I take on that challenge – have I got maps and charts to assist me?'

'Have I got, or can I get, enough food and drink to sustain us?'

These are just some of the issues that therapists may take to supervision.

Some therapists are reluctant to avail themselves of regular supervision for many reasons, although the reason given is very often 'lack of time 'and 'pressure of work' – people are so busy helping others that they neglect their own needs.

I believe that supervision is cost-effective in that it brings to the client clarity and focus on the work being undertaken. It both identifies and builds on the skills of the supervisee and stops her feeling isolated, so reducing stress. Some work I am undertaking indicates that a person having regular effective supervision tends to have lower rates of sick leave and stays at the 'coal face' longer in career terms.

When working with sufferers of PTSD, in addition to debriefing I would recommend that supervision be sought fortnightly for a minimum period of an hour. This would both contribute to safe practice and assist in the development of the worker, which in turn reflects itself in the client–therapist relationship.

There are several comprehensive books on supervision now available (Hawkins and Shohet 1989, Proctor 1988, Heron 1974. See also Chapter 8, Further reading), providing different models to suit different people. In this chapter, however, I intend to write more specifically on supervision for dramatherapists working with individuals and their families suffering from the effects of PTSD.

The supervisee

The therapist knows that for a good treatment outcome the client has to fully acknowledge the problem and want assistance to overcome it. For supervision to be effective the supervisee needs to be committed to it and know that it is an integral part of the work she does.

She must build a relationship of trust with her supervisor. A respect for the way the supervisor works is important, although the supervisor does not need to be a dramatherapist as a different perspective can open things up somewhat. The supervisee needs space as safe as that which she provides for her clients, to enable her to be fully open with her supervisor and not to censor the more distressing details of her work.

The supervisor

The supervisor needs to be familiar with and experienced in working with clients with acute and chronic Post Traumatic Stress or must have experience in grief therapy. She should also have received formal training in supervision and be clear about its elements, boundaries and purpose. Just as an untrained 'counsellor' can become an 'advice-giver', an untrained supervisor can fall into the trap of saying 'you should have done it this way' or, in other words, 'I could have done it better'. The purpose of the supervision is to facilitate the supervisee to remain and grow more effective in the work with her clients.

Within the health service and social service departments in the UK there is a tendency for the manager to be the supervisor. This may be difficult on several accounts. The supervision session may be focused on hierarchical, organisational issues, which can put both parties on the defensive and leave little time for process supervision. Other distractions occurring in the work setting may mean frequent cancellations of supervision sessions. The internal dynamics of a team may be ignored. If everyone is doing the same sort of work, the team may become introspective and subjective. It seems sensible for an external supervisor to be available and this will also free managers to focus more upon management duties and keep a global view of service provision and development.

When working with therapists who have clients in treatment for PTSD, the supervisor has an important role in accepting and creating room to hear repetition of grim details. I have observed supervisors who have cut the supervisee short by saying things such as 'I get the picture – there's no need to elaborate'. (Who would respond to a client in that way?) There is every need to elaborate and then explore what it means to the therapist and how they are to work with it, with their client. The key concepts of treatment for PTSD (see Chapter 5) can be applied during supervision. It should be acknowledged that just as some therapists find it difficult, and choose not to work with certain client groups, so some supervisors may find it too difficult to supervise workers who are involved in PTSD work.

Trained supervisors are normally aware and committed to receiving supervision themselves – the first prerequisite of being a good supervisor is being able actively to arrange good supervision for yourself. A useful question to ask yourself is: 'Am I currently receiving adequate supervision, both for the other work I'm doing and for being a supervisor?'

The relationship between supervisee and supervisor

This relationship can also serve as a model for the therapist–client relationship.

Mutual regard and co-operation are important. The supervisee should be proactive in stating what she requires from the supervisor, rather than being a passive recipient. A contract and regular review and evaluation of the supervisory session and dynamics can bring clarity. Often what happens in the 'here and now' of that relationship reflects on what is happening in the client–therapist setting. Proctor (1988) writes: 'It will also be the case that a worker often comes to supervision stressed, anxious, angry, afraid. It is our assumption that only if he feels safe enough to talk about these uncomfortable feelings, and fully acknowledge them for himself will he be "cleared" to re-evaluate his practice.'

When working with PTSD if a supervisor 'blocks' intensive emotions that the therapist may be feeling by changing focus, this may be paralleled in the therapy setting. If the therapist is unsupported, for how long will she be able to support those she works with?

Boundaries in supervision

Issues such as frequency of meetings, length of sessions, contingency arrangements and the fee (if applicable) should be laid down in the pre-arranged contract (see Appendix).

Another boundary that emerges is that between supervision and therapy. When dealing with intense emotions and looking at issues of counter-transference, the supervisee may well come into contact with her own suppressed material, or something she felt she had 'worked through' may emerge with a different intensity. The supervisor has to enquire what effect this has on the therapeutic relationship or wider work setting. What effect does it have on the supervisee's ability to practice? Various interventions such as 'empty chair' work, spectograms or 'doubling' may facilitate these emotions, helping the supervisee identify her difficulty. The supervisor can then, providing a supportive, safe, atmosphere, ask the person what bearing it has on her perception of the work. The focus, therefore, goes on to integral personal issues for a while, but then returns to the work and to where the supervisee will go with it. If the re-stimulated personal material is in need of more facilitation and exploration, the supervisee can be encouraged by the supervisor to get some counselling or therapy to assist this.

Hawkins and Shohet (1989) put it succinctly: 'Supervision sessions should always start from exploring issues from work and should end with looking at where the supervisee goes next with the work that has been explored.' (p.45)

In crisis work the client has to be encouraged to keep to the task rather than diffusing the process by bringing in unrelated issues as a subconscious means of avoidance. The same can be said of supervision of therapy involving traumatic material: by refocusing on the work-related issues the supervisor prevents this occurring, although she may validate the other material in brief.

Group supervision

If there are co-workers involved in the facilitation of a dramatherapy group, or if there is a small team working together in the treatment of people with PTSD, a supervision group with an external supervisor may be useful. Such a group ideally requires a minimum of three members and no more than seven.

Before undertaking to work with the group, the supervisor needs to elicit from them that which is expected, such as:

- What is the purpose of your group?
- What do you want to give to each other?
- What do you hope to receive from each other?
- What do you expect from me?
- Why have you called me in now? (Often this can be reactionary – for example if the team dynamics are in chaos – and it is as well for the supervisor to be prepared.)
- What do you want to be different?

This process helps each group member to be pro-active in the contract-making and gives them all an opportunity to voice differences and similarities in expectations. It also makes them aware of the need for their active participation in identifying their needs in the supervision.

Group supervision is more economical in finance, time and expertise, although it is hoped that this is not the main consideration. Another benefit is that it can become a positive, team-building experience for a group, if they are open enough to express their fears and anxieties, and generous enough to offer support to one another. The supervisees may come from a variety of backgrounds – social, race, culture, age or gender – allowing for different perspectives to be shared and reflected in client practice. Finally, other group members may challenge collusions between the supervisor and supervisee; for example, some client material may touch on some conflicts which are unresolved for both parties and which, in a one-to-one setting, they may both pass over. However, in group supervision another group member may take the chance to draw attention to these dynamics, and so cause them and their effects to be explored further.

A disadvantage of group supervision is when the group dynamics result in games such as 'Hunt the patient', 'Let's play therapists', and 'Who's the best therapist?' being played out. If the dynamics become superimposed, the group can become totally self-absorbed, almost to the exclusion of any interest in the clients. A skilled supervisor with a good knowledge of group dynamics will not be daunted by this (although it may be a covert expression of hostility towards her). If the situation has descended to this level, only by addressing it will the impasse be removed and work resumed. Heron (1974) reminds us that if a group is too similar in terms of types of client, theoretical approach and level of accomplishment, learning and challenge is limited and there is a danger in promoting 'consensus collusion'. This is my reason for not favouring peer supervision when working with PTSD: the work with clients is intense and difficult at times, and these emotions may be undiluted in a peer group supervision setting.

An obvious advantage of using a group supervision model is that what takes place in a therapy group can be reconstructed through role-play and the supervisees can experience different ways of being, different group roles, can gain feedback from other members regarding how they felt in their assigned roles, and can be offered different ideas on ways of proceeding.

There are four elements within the supervision of therapists working with PTSD: educational; process; managerial; and supportive. The *educational* element may take on prominence in a training group: the supervisor shares her knowledge and latest research with the supervisees to strengthen and enhance their knowledge base and encourage them to seek more information. The aim is to build up the supervisees' confidence and skill. The issue of *process* is particularly important and involves looking at what the therapist felt in relation to what took place whether she feels that that is being paralleled in the 'here and now', and encourages self-awareness and acknowledgement of the effect of the client on the therapist/supervisee. It is also an easier way for therapists who are not familiar with receiving supervision to understand the importance and relevance of doing so, in order for them to continue effectively in this sort of work. The *managerial* element occurs depending on whether or not the supervisor works for the organisation and has managerial responsibility. It should help the supervisee to identify priorities and to use resources to their greatest effectiveness, and should identify good practices, provide positive feedback and remedy deficits. It is also useful for keeping track of practices, for example ensuring that adequate records are being maintained (these are often requested in compensation hearings). The *supportive* element should be infused into the proceedings. An extremely useful tool that may be used in a supportive way, I find, is humour. This needs to be handled with sensitivity, and should never be at the expense of others or oneself, but there are times when it is good to laugh. However, if I am to try to show my clients that it is good to feel happy and to come in and out of their grief (Hawkins and Shohet 1989), then I need to know how to be happy, and to be able to laugh and see paradoxes. Earnest trainee therapists and those who have forgotten how to do this, also can be reminded that it can help with healing. Lifting the mood can help us to see things in a different light.

Individual supervision

In order for us to take care of others, we need to learn to take care of ourselves. If we do not do this then we risk projecting our own needs on to our clients. We begin first to deny our personal difficulties, then to deny our feelings and ultimately to deny our own humanity – or is it humility? Is an automaton any use as a role model? Availing ourselves of suitable supervision is our way of saying 'I need support, nurturing, a guide, as well.' In the caring professions it is common to encourage clients to seek space for themselves, yet to feel we don't deserve it for ourselves.

The busier and more pressured I feel with client work, the more I know it is essential to keep my supervision appointments. The model of supervision I use, both as supervisor and supervisee, is the Process Model of Supervision described by Hawkins and Shohet (1989). This model divides supervision styles into two main categories, which can be used in conjunction with one another:

1. *Supervision that pays attention directly to the therapy matrix through the supervisee and supervisor reflecting together on the reports, written notes or tape recordings of the therapy sessions.*

   This can be further explained by describing the three modes that comprise this approach:

   a) Reflection on the content of the therapy session. This focuses closely on the actual happenings during the session, i.e. how the patient centred himself, what he shared, what he withheld, how the therapy is progressing and how one session has related to another. The aim of this supervision is to help the therapist look at what the client wants to do, the choices that he or she is making and how these choices relate to the client's life.

   b) Exploration of the modes of working that the therapist is using. Here, the supervisor pays attention to what strategies the therapist has been using, how helpful they have been, and what other intervention could be used or further developed. This sort of supervision leads to an increase in both the therapist's levels of skills and her confidence in what she is doing and why she is doing it.

   c) Exploration of the therapy process and relationship. The supervisor pays attention to both the conscious and unconscious processes that are apparently occurring within the therapy session. As an outsider, the supervisor is able to look at how the session progressed, any themes that recur with that particular client, any metaphors that have perhaps not been picked up by the therapist, and any changes in the voice or posture of the therapist, or, in the case of tapes being listened to, in the voice of the client. For example, a therapist recounting a response to an intervention that she made may suddenly sit forward on her chair and become animated, or alternatively may slump back and appear negative. This can be explored with the supervisor and may provide an insight in to the dynamics of the therapeutic relationship – perhaps the therapist is mirroring the behaviour of the client.

2. *Supervision that pays attention to the therapy matrix through how that system is reflected in the 'here and now' experiences of the supervision process.*

    Again, there are three modes comprising this approach:

    a) Focus on the therapist's counter-transference. The supervisor focuses on whatever is still being carried by the therapist both consciously and unconsciously from the therapy session and the client. For example, a therapist worked with people who had been abused, and during her supervision session continually remarked on how she felt put down, let down, trampled on, and powerless within her organisation. On further exploration of this, it became apparent that she had not been able to 'download' from a session with a client, but instead had taken on many of the feelings that the client had projected. In addition, she had been abused by incessant demands from the client and had been able to distance herself from this.

    b) Focus on the 'here and now' process. This looks at any mirroring or paralleling within the supervision session of what happened during the therapy session: this is quite a common phenomenon, which is definitely worth exploring. For example, I have supervised someone working with adolescents, who had started to mirror the adolescent behaviour, until we explored the 'here and now' process and what it all actually meant.

    c) Focus on the supervisor's transference. Here, the supervisor provides the therapist with feedback on the images, thoughts and emotions that have occurred. Such a reflection may not happen during the therapy session, but can be picked up by the supervisor.

As supervisors, this model, which seems to me to be a supervisee-centred and integrated way of providing supervision, both allows us to be aware of our own strengths and weaknesses within the supervision process, and enables us consciously to change modes in order to shed more light on what is occurring. Often when supervising someone working with PTSD, the first category in which the supervisee is recounting the therapy session is the most useful one, as it allows for the debriefing if the therapist, which is vital in this type of work. I believe that it is only when the therapist is clear of this material that she is able to concentrate and listen to deeper explanation during the supervision. The use of metaphor is also helpful here, as it allows the therapist to distance him- or herself from the traumatic material, and therefore further explore its meaning, in just the same way that she encourages her clients to do. Equally, when a session has been particularly difficult and traumatic for the therapist, it can be useful to provide materials such as candles, carrier bags, clay, a selection of cushions and so on: just as we encourage clients to externalise some of their feelings, it is important to allow therapists to do the same. Many dramatherapy methods may also be used to explore issues in supervision. The creation of safe space, free from interruption, is a prerequisite.

Case study

SK attended for her fifth supervision session. She was a mental health worker with several years' experience. For the past year she had been working with clients fulfilling the criteria for a diagnosis of PTSD. She now accepted the supervisory process and wondered how she had previously managed. In this session she came in and sat down and, although smiling, she had a guarded body posture and seemed preoccupied.

Supervisee: I'm not sure what I want to bring today. I'm really tired; there's so much going on:

Supervisor: You look tense.

Supervisee: It's the client I'm seeing later; there's so much going on I'm sure, but she just blocks me.

Supervisor: Is that the client you brought to supervision two weeks ago? You felt she was near a disclosure.

Supervisee: Yes [*becoming more animated*]. She told me she had been raped during her holiday abroad. She spoke to me about how relieved she was to have told me, as she'd kept it to herself, saying she had only been mugged [*trivialising as part of denial*]. She cried a lot and I extended the session to make sure she felt safe to leave the space.

Supervisor: It's good that she has managed to name what's happened to her and that you were able to give her the time. You feel she blocks you. [*Am I blocking supervisee? Give space.*]

Supervisee: It was easier when she was. I know I need to listen to her story, but I don't know how to. Perhaps I can use some projective work with the doll figures and choice of objects on the sand tray, it's difficult... [*Long silence. Supervisee looks tearful.*]

Supervisor: You say it's difficult, you don't know how to...

Supervisee: We all have stories [*looks at floor*].

Supervisor: What about yours?

Supervisee: I thought I'd dealt with it, but its all come back to me.

Supervisor: Do you want to tell me yours? [*gesturing to figures and sand tray*]

Supervisee: [*Grasped some figures and moved to tray where she worked intently for five minutes. She then went into some detail about a rape that was inflicted on her about two years ago and that she had rationalised. This lasted for thirty minutes.*]

Supervisor: [*Facilitation minimal. Held supervisee for a while. Assisted supervisee in de-roling figures.*]

Supervisee: Why couldn't I see that before? I feel I can breathe deeply again. I know I need to look at it more. I'll contact the rape help line I think.

Supervisor: You look less tense now. How do you feel? [*Keep boundaries between supervision and therapy.*]

Supervisee: Okay. I'm not so worried about seeing my client now. I was scared I'd block her.

Supervisor: You're okay. How are you going to work with her? [*reaffirming supervisee as a therapist*]

Supervisee: I'm going to help her find a way to tell her story.

This was an emotional supervisional session that went into a personal issue that was having a direct effect on the therapist's ability to proceed with a client. By acknowledging and naming that issue she was then freed to proceed with clients' work and to continue on the journey.

If a therapist is feeling distressed, for example by a death that has been described to her, she may find it helpful to be able to pay her own tribute to the deceased person before moving on, and she may be encouraged to do this by playwork or other artistic work, which enables her to express the feelings that she may otherwise keep inside. It may be that after the supervision session the supervisor will also feel the need to do similarly.

Further reading

Cherniss, C. (1980) *Staff Burnout*. Beverly Hills: Sage.

Eldewich, J. and Broadsky, A. (1980) *Burn-Out*. New York: Human Sciences.

Hess, A.K. (ed) (1980) *Psychotherapy Supervision: Theory, Research and Practice*. New York: Wiley.

Langs, R. (1983) *The Supervision Experience*. New York: Jason Aronson.

Shainberg, D. (1983).'Teaching therapists to be with their clients', in Westwood, J. (ed). *Awakening the Heart*. Colorado: Shambhala.

CHAPTER 9

Conclusion

The recognition and treatment of PTSD is becoming more wide-spread. Consequently, through experience, research and knowledge, therapists are developing their skills accordingly. It is hoped that this book will assist dramatherapists in their work with people suffering from this problem. It is intended to provide a framework or guide for the journey the dramatherapist and client will share.

Dramatherapy is particularly useful in cases where other treatments have not been successful due to the person's reluctance to engage or his resistance to 'feeling' any emotion. One of the effects of a traumatic incident can be that the person affected becomes an expert at giving factual, detached accounts of the event to agencies such as the media, police and lawyers, and as a result becomes unable to talk about it in any other way. If, as a dramatherapist, you are receiving a verbal account of the event in this way, you should at a suitable point enquire how the person actually feels. Dramatherapy, with its use of methods such as metaphor, story, spectograms, and symbolism, can, paradoxically, provide the distance necessary for the person or group to explore in depth how they are affected and to look at solutions to their difficulties.

The order of treatment I would recommend (and the research I am undertaking confirms this) is:

1. *Initial assessment*. This provides a baseline for all future work. It determines whether the person is best suited to individual or group therapy, and introduces him to creative ways of working. Careful record-keeping is vital at this stage, both for future reference and, should it be required at a later stage, in any legal action. It is important to ascertain in the assessment whether there has been any previous trauma – one may mask the other.

2. *Debriefing/normalisation.* This should be carried out as close to the time of the incident as possible. I and other colleagues have found that this is sometimes all the treatment that people require, even if it does not come until some considerable time after the incident. Debriefing helps people to realise that their reactions are normal, which can allay their fears and put them back in charge of their lives.

3. *Key concepts in treatment.* These should be followed as described in Chapter 5. Clients often find it helpful to be given an outline of these concepts so that they know what to expect, and so that they are more able to give informed consent to treatment. The presence of such a structure, together with a specific goal, certainly seems to be of help.

4. *Supervision.* I include this under treatment, as it needs to run in tandem. It cannot be emphasised enough that supervision, preferably by someone with knowledge of both PTSD and dramatherapy, is essential, both in order to ensure a quality service for the clients and to prevent the dramatherapist becoming a casualty of the process.

The length of time people require in therapy is dependent to some extent on how long they have had PTSD and how it has affected their lives. It seems to vary from as little as six sessions to as long as two years.

A recent exciting development in dramatherapy is 'brief therapy', which certainly seems to be useful in the treatment of PTSD, where the aim is to restore the person to optimal functioning as quickly as possible. Work on brief dramatherapy is currently being further developed and consolidated by Alida Gersie and others (Gersie 1993 and in press).

A by-product of dramatherapy treatment for PTSD is often a reawakening or discovery of creativity, and many clients have gone on to write (either fiction, poetry, or of their experiences), sculpt, paint or engage in another artistic activity (including drama). On meeting some of them again, or hearing from them after they have recovered, it is a joy to learn of their achievements.

I hope this book provides an insight into PTSD, and makes it possible to lessen the chances of its development following an encounter with an incident outside the range of normal human experience and, where it has occurred, to heal the wounds.

Sample Supervision Contract

Confidentiality

The parties respect the confidential nature of material being brought for supervision. It may be, though, that some issues that arise will need to be discussed further in the supervisor's supervision: if this arises the supervisor will discuss it first with the supervisee. The supervisor is guided by the UKCC Code of Confidentiality. This contract is written for nurses, other professions including Dramatherapy will be guided by their professional bodies and boundaries specified by them. A copy of which is available. Personal material that is brought to supervision will remain confidential, if an issue is serious then the supervisor will discuss with the supervisee where this should be taken.

Time boundaries

The time of the session will be clearly specified and decided upon between the supervisor and the supervisee. This will normally be an hour but may be changed with notice and negotiation. If the supervisee has to cancel a session, then notice of this would be appreciated. If an emergency arises and supervision has to be abandoned, this will be treated as an unusual occurrence, and another supervision session arranged at a mutually convenient time. If the supervisee arrives late to the session, it may not be possible to have the full length as previously arranged because of other commitments of the supervisor.

Safe boundaries

The space where the supervisor and supervisee meet will be mutually agreed and acceptable. It is important that it is quiet and free from interruption.

There are four components of supervision:

- Managerial
- Educational
- Supportive
- Debriefing

It is recognised that sometimes one of these components may be more emphasised than the others; again the focus can be looked at by the supervisor and supervisee to suit the need of the supervisee. It is hoped that the supervisee will be guided by the supervisor. For the purpose of clarifying where supervision ends and therapy begins, it is helpful to remember that supervision sessions should always start by exploring issues from work and should end by looking at where the supervisee goes next with the work that has been explored. Personal material may come into the session if it is directly affecting, or being affected by, the work discussed, or if it is affecting the supervision relationship. It is necessary at times to look at the relationship between the supervisor and the supervisee, as this is often a reflection of what is happening in the therapist–client relationship.

Ideally, supervision should allow for the supervisee

- to have space to reflect upon the content and process of her work
- to develop understanding and skills within the work
- to receive information in another perspective concerning one's work
- to receive both content and process feedback
- to be validated and supported both as a person and a worker
- to ensure that, as a person and a worker, one is not left to carry unnecessarily difficulties, problems and projections alone

- to have space to explore and express personal distress, restimulation, transference or counter-transference that may be brought up by the work
- to plan and utilise better personal and professional resources
- to be proactive rather than reactive
- to ensure quality of work.

It is hoped that the supervisee will feel able to bring issues to the supervisor, and, if she feels any of the above areas are not being looked at in enough depth, to voice this so that it may be remedied.

Linda Winn © 1992

References

ACAS (1989) *Survey of Occupational Stress Factors in the London Ambulance Service*. London: ACAS

American Psychiatric Association (1987) *Diagnostic Statistical Manual of Mental Disorders 3rd edition*. Washington DC: The American Psychiatric Association.

British Association of Dramatherapists (1991) *Code of Ethics*. Fife: BADth.

Brook, P. (1972) *The Empty Space*. London: Penguin.

Cassim, N. (1986) 'We know love', the return of the Aamasi bird. In J. Gruchy *Cry Justice*. London: Collins Flame.

Casson, J. (1991) Developing a dramatherapy studio. *Dramatherapy Newsletter* Summer 1991, 7–9.

Cherniss, C. (1980) *Staff Burnout*. Beverly Hills: Sage.

Figley, C.R. and Sprenkle, D.H. (1978) Delayed stress response syndrome; family therapy indications. *Journal of Marriage and Family Counselling*. 27, 53–60.

General Practice Research Unit (1978) *General Health Questionnaire*. Windsor: NFER Nelson.

Gersie, A. (1983) Storytelling and its link with the unconscious: Journey into myth. *British Journal of Dramatherapy*, 7, 1.

Gersie, A. (1991) *Storymaking in Bereavement*. London: Jessica Kingsley Publishers.

Gersie, A. (1993) Newsletter. *Dramatherapy* Autumn 1993, 8.

Gersie, A. (in press) *Dramatic Approaches to Brief Therapy*. London: Jessica Kingsley Publishers.

Gersie, A. and King, N. (1990) *Storymaking in Education and Therapy*. London: Jessica Kingsley Publishers.

Ghandi (1946) *Hindustan Standard*, 8 December.

Grigsby, J.P. (1987) The use of imagery in the treatment of Post Traumatic Stress Disorder. *Journal of Nervous Mental Disability*. 175, 55–59.

Guggenbuhl, C.A. (1971) *Power in the Helping Professions*. Dallas: Spring.

Hawkins, P. and Shohet, R. (1989) *Supervision in the Helping Professions.* Milton Keynes: Open University Press.

Helmann, C. (1984) *Culture, Health and Illness.* Bristol, London: Wright PSG.

Heron, J. (1974) *Reciprocal Counselling.* Guildford: University of Surrey.

Hoban, R. (1979) *Gentleman David. The Dancing Tigers* – A red fox picture book. London: Arrow Books.

Horwood, W. (1990) *Duncton Found.* London: Arrow Books.

Ingemann, B.S. *Through the Night of Doubt and Sorrow.* Hymn trans by S. Baring-Gould.

Jennings, E. (1986) John of the Cross. In *Collected Poems.* Manchester Carcanet Press.

Jennings, S. (1986) *Creative Drama in Groupwork.* Bicester: Winslow Press.

Jennings, S. (1987) Dramatherapy and groups. In S. Jennings (ed.) *Dramatherapy Theory and Practice for Teachers and Clinicians.* London: Routledge.

Jennings, S. (1990) *Dramatherapy with Families, Groups and Individuals.* London: Jessica Kingsley Publishers.

Jupp, H. (unpubl) *Anxiety Management Package.* Circulated by Hilary Jupp.

Kalff, D. (1980) *Sand Play – A Psychotherapeutic Approach to the Psyche.* Boston, MA: Sigo Press.

Keane, M.K. and Kaloupek, D.G. (1982) Imaginal flooding in the treatment of PTSD. *Journal of Consultant Clinical Psychology* 50. p.138–140.

Keubler-Ross, E. (1970) *On Death and Dying.* New York: Macmillian Press.

Kfir, N. (1989) *Crisis Intervention Verbatim.* New York: Hemisphere Publishing Corporation.

Landy, R. (1986) *Dramatherapy: Concepts and Practice.* Springfield: Charles C. Thomas

Langley, D. and Langley, G. (1983) *Dramatherapy and Psychiatry.* Beckenham: Croom Helm.

Leick, N. and Daudsen-Nielsen, M. (1991) *Healing Pain: Attachment, Loss and Grief Therapy.* London: Routledge.

Murphy, S.A. (1987) Self efficiency and social support mediators of stress on mental health following a natural disaster. *Kango Kenky* Vol 20 (4),é 360–369.

Noori, C. (1979) 'we know love': The return of the Admasi Bird. *Staffrider,* March, 336–7.

NUPE (1991) Evidence to the Hillsborough Inquiry.

Proctor, B. (1988) *Supervision: A Working Alliance.* East Sussex: Alexia Publications.

Raphael, B. (1986) *When Disaster Strikes: How Individuals and Communities Cope with Catastrophe*. New York: Basic Books.

Roethke, T. (1975) The Abyss. In *Collected Poems of Theodore Roethke*. New York: Doubleday and Co.

Rosetti, C. (1970) If only. In E. Jennings *A Choice of Christina Rosetti's Verse*. London: Faber and Faber.

Shuttleworth, R. (1990) Notes from a lecture given by R. Shuttleworth at the Annual Dramatherapy Conference, Manchester.

Tournier, P. (1965) *The Adventure of Living*. Sussex: Highland Books.

Turner, V. (1969) *The Ritual Process*. London: Routledge and Kegan Paul.

Turner, V. (1976) *Forest of Symbols*. New York: Cornell University Press.

Turner, V. (1982) From ritual to theatre. *Performing Arts Journal*.

UKCC (1992) *Code of Professional Conduct for the Nurse; Midwife and Health Visitor*. UKCC, 23 Portland Place, London W1N 3AF.

Van Gennep, A. (1960) *Rites De Passage* London: Routledge, Kegan Paul.

Watzlawick, P. (1978) *The Language of Change*. New York: Basic Books.

Wolfe, T. (1983) *The Autobiography of an American Novelist* (edited by L. Field). Cambridge: Harvard University Press.

Wright, B. (1993) *Caring in Crisis, 2nd edition*. Edinburgh: Churchill Livingstone.